All-STAR Phonics

Level A

Senior Author
Alvin Granowsky, Ed.D.
Educational Consultant
Former Director of Reading and Language Arts
Greensboro, North Carolina, and Dallas, Texas

Contributing Author
Claudia Cornett, Ph.D.
Professor Emerita
Education/Literacy Methodology
Wittenberg University
Springfield, Ohio

SRA
A Division of The McGraw·Hill Companies
Columbus, Ohio

Program Reviewers

David Wallace
Associate Superintendent
Noblesville School District
Noblesville, Indiana

Linda Bronstein
Classroom Teacher
Hartford School District
West Hartford, Connecticut

Mary Brandenburg
Classroom Teacher
Lawton Chiles Elementary School
Gainesville, Florida

Jennifer Vasile
Classroom Teacher
Abraham Lincoln Elementary School
Glen Ellyn, Illinois

Linda Carle
Classroom Teacher
Bonsack Elementary School
Roanoke, Virginia

Lois Zercher
Assistant Superintendent
Lemoore Union Elementary School
Lemoore, California

Acknowledgments

Grateful acknowledgment is given to the following publishers and copyright owners for permissions granted to reprint selections from their publications. All possible care has been taken to trace ownership and secure permission for each selection included. In case of any errors or omissions, the Publisher will be pleased to make suitable acknowledgments in future editions.

"Cat Kisses" copyright © 1974 by Bobbi Katz, copyright renewed 1996. Used with permission of Bobbi Katz who controls all rights.

"Hamsters" Text copyright © 1969, 1996 by Marci Ridlon McGill from SUN THROUGH THE WINDOW by Marci Ridlon McGill. Published by Wordsong/Boyds Mills Press, Inc. Reprinted by permission.

"Little Seeds" from THE WINDS THAT COME FROM FAR AWAY by ELSE HOMELUND MINARIK. TEXT COPYRIGHT © 1964 BY ELSE HOMELUND MINARIK. ILLUSTRATION COPYRIGHT © 1964 BY JOAN PHYLLIS BERG. Used by permission of HarperCollins Publishers.

"Seed, Sprout, Flower" by Helen H. Moore from PERFECT POEMS FOR TEACHING PHONICS by Deborah Ellermeyer et al. Published by Scholastic Professional Books, a division of Scholastic Inc. Copyright © 1997 by Helen H. Moore. Reprinted by permission of Scholastic, Inc.

"Good-Bye, Six-Hello, Seven" Reprinted with the permission of Atheneum Books for Young Readers, an imprint of Simon & Schuster Children's Publishing Division from IF I WERE IN CHARGE OF THE WORLD AND OTHER WORRIES by Judith Viorst. Text copyright © 1981 Judith Viorst.

From THE LORAX by Dr. Seuss, ® and copyright © by Dr. Seuss Enterprises, L.P. 1917, renewed 1999. Used by permission of Random House Children's Books, a division of Random House, Inc.

"poem for rodney" from SPIN A SOFT BLACK SONG REVISED EDITION by Nikki Giovanni, illustrated by George Martins. Copyright © 1971, 1985 by Nikki Giovanni. Reprinted by permission of Farrar, Straus and Giroux, LLC.

"Fish" from THE LLAMA WHO HAD NO PAJAMA, copyright © 1959 and renewed 1987 by Mary Ann Hoberman, reprinted by permission of Harcourt, Inc.

Joanna Cole for "Driving to the Beach." Copyright © 1973 by Joanna Cole.

"Daylight Saving Time" Copyright © 1966 by Phyllis McGinley. First appeared in WONDERFUL TIME published by J.B. Lippincott. Reprinted by permission of Curtis Brown, Ltd.

"Bad Timing" by Arden Davidson. Used by permission of the author.

www.sra4kids.com

SRA/McGraw-Hill

A Division of The ***McGraw-Hill*** *Companies*

Send all inquiries to:
SRA/McGraw-Hill
8787 Orion Place
Columbus, OH 43240-4027

Printed in the United States of America.

ISBN 0-07-572559-2

3 4 5 6 QPD 07 06

Table of Contents

Unit 2 Continued

Unit 3 Short Vowel Sounds

Unit Theme: Can I Help?

Unit 3 Continued

Unit 4 Long Vowel Sounds

Unit Theme: When I Grow Up

Unit 4 Continued

Unit 5 Consonant Blends

Unit Theme: At the Store

Unit 6 Consonant Digraphs

Unit Theme: At the Seashore

Unit 7 Word Studies

Unit Theme: All about Time

Unit 7 Continued

The Best Pets

Hamsters

by Marci Ridlon

Hamsters are the nicest things
That anyone could own.
I like them even better than
Some dogs I have known.

Their fur is soft, their faces nice.
They're small when they are grown.
And they sit inside your pocket
When you are all alone.

On My Mind

What is the funniest pet you have heard about?

All-STARs at Home

Dear Family,

Your child is beginning a new program, *SRA All-STAR Phonics.* This program helps your child learn about letters, sounds, and words. These skills are important as your child learns to read.

Each unit has a particular skill focus and a special theme. The theme will give your child opportunities to use his or her new skills while learning about a topic. In Unit 1, your child will learn to identify the letters of the alphabet while discussing "The Best Pets."

Here are some fun activities you can share with your child:

★ Sing "The Alphabet Song" with your child. Take turns, each saying one line at a time. You can also sing the song by letting your child say a letter and you say the one that follows, etc.

★ Invite your child to cut large letters from newspaper or magazine ads. Help him or her paste the letters on paper to make an alphabet chart.

★ Look for alphabet books at the library. We suggest:

- *Chicka Chicka Boom Boom* by Bill Martin Jr. and John Archambault, Simon & Schuster, 1989.
- *Eating the Alphabet: Fruits and Vegetables from A to Z* by Lois Ehlert, Harcourt, 1994.

I Can Do It!

Draw a line to match each letter.

1

2

3

4

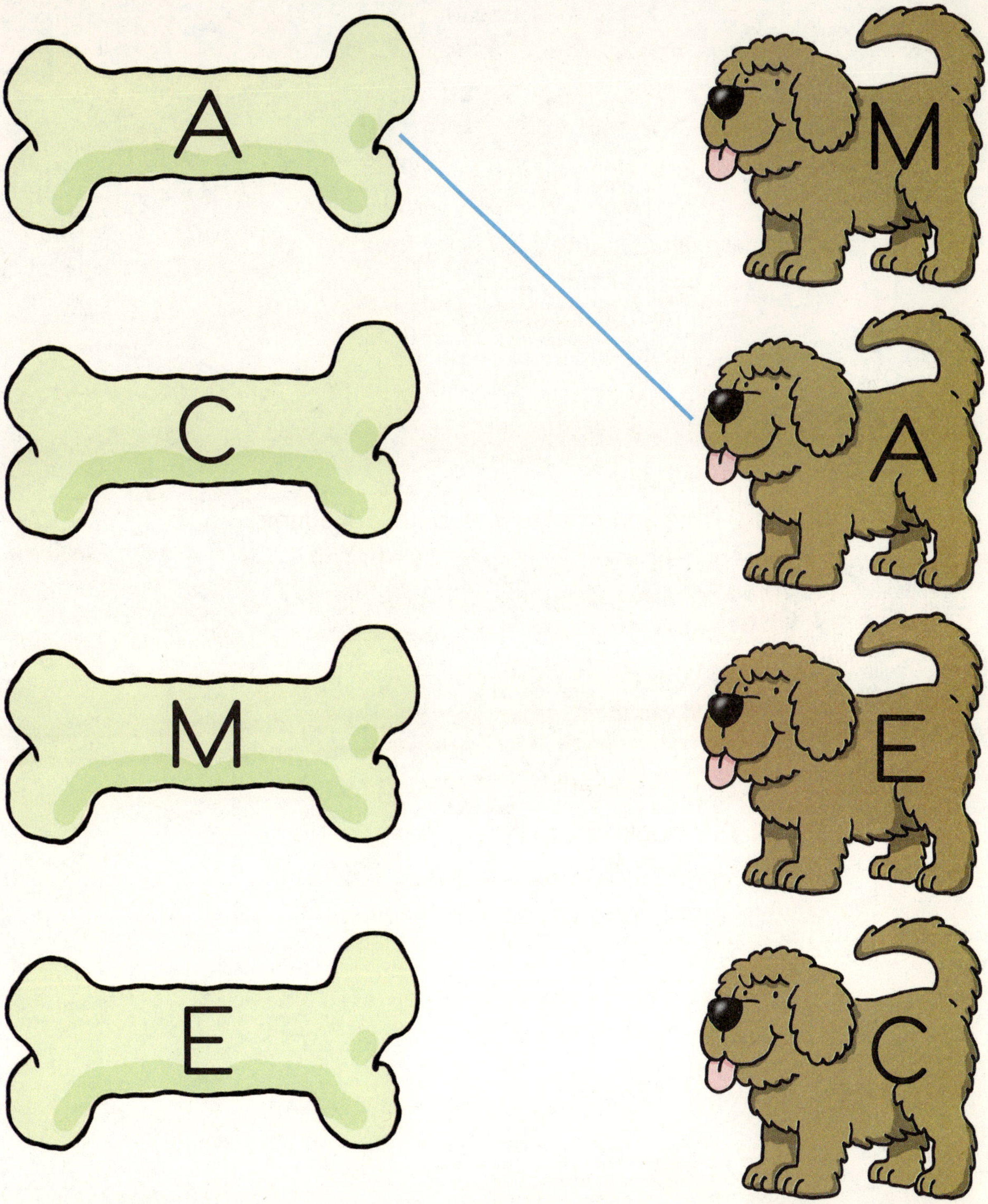

Riddle Time What kind of dog makes a good lunch?

Answer: A hot dog!

I Can Do It!

Lesson 1: Matching Uppercase Letters

Draw a line to match each letter.

I Can Do It!

Draw a line to match each letter.

b

p

n

b

p

n

Think and Link Which lowercase letters above have circles in them?

Lesson 2: Matching Lowercase Letters

Look at the letters on the colored fish. **Find** the fish with the same letter and **color** them to match.

I Can Do It!

Say the name of each picture.
Circle the two pictures that rhyme in each row.

1

2

3

4

I Can Do It!

Lesson 3: Rhyming Sounds

Say the name of each picture in each set. **Draw** a line from the top picture to each picture that rhymes with it.

Rhyme Time What words can you think of that rhyme with *hot*?

I Can Do It!

Say the names of the pictures in each set. **Color** the picture with the same beginning sound as the first picture.

1

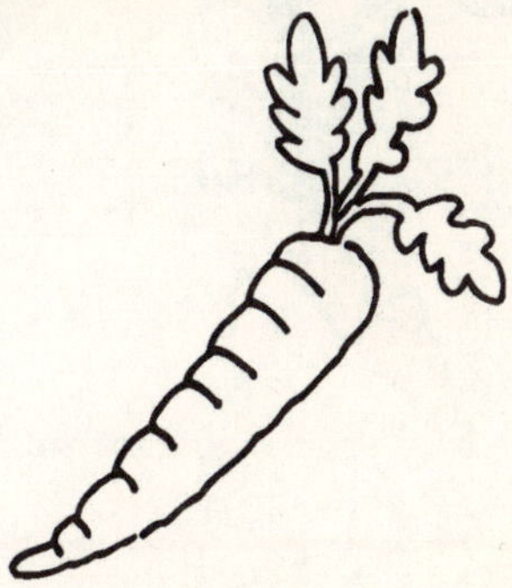

2

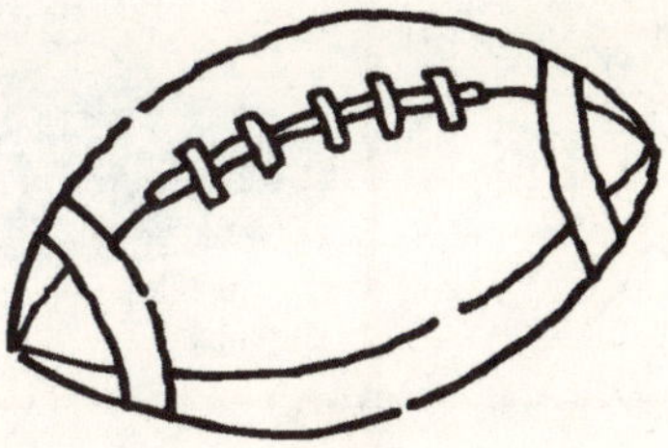

3

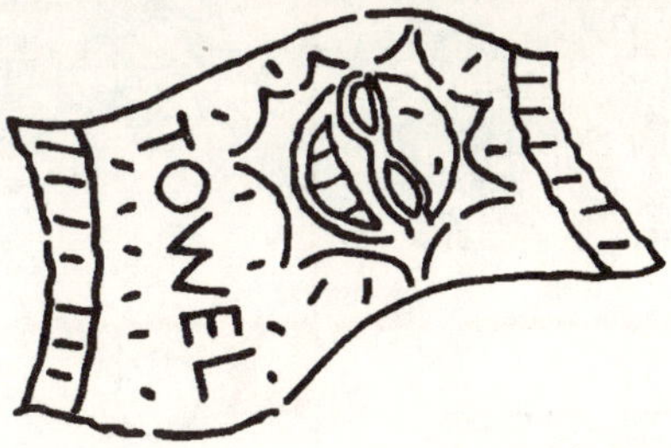

4

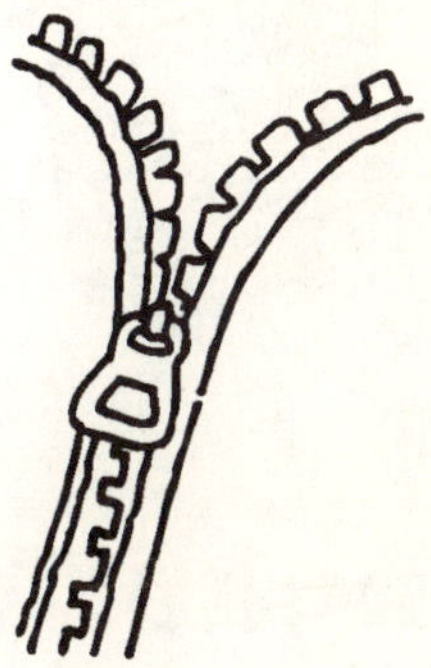

I Can Do It!

Lesson 4: Beginning Sounds

Say the names of the pictures in each set. **Fill in** the circle if the pictures begin with the same sound.

1 ● 

2 ○ 

3 ○ 

4 ○ 

5 ○ 

6 ○ 

7 ○ 

8 ○ 

Tongue Twister Casey cooked a can of carrots.

Write the letters on the lines.

A a

B b

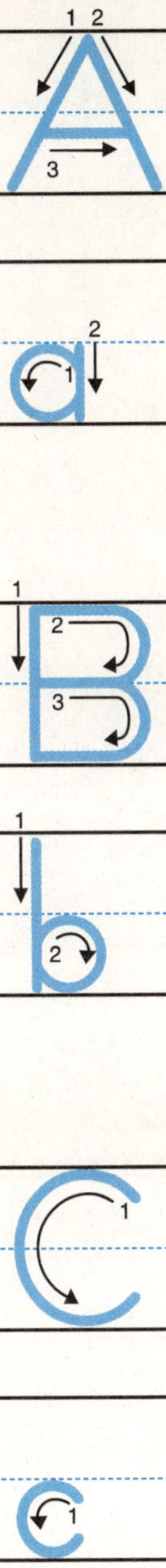

C c

Think and Link Which uppercase letters above have curves?

I Can Do It!

Lesson 6: Dd, Ee, Ff

Write the letters on the lines.

D

d

E

e

F

f

Tongue Twister Fat frogs fly fast.

I Can Do It!

Write the letters on the lines.

G

g

H

h

I

i

Big Idea Why do you think horses make good pets?

Review

Lesson 8: Review Uppercase and Lowercase Letters

Draw a line to match each pair of letters.

Lesson 9: Jj, Kk, Ll

I Can Do It!

Write the letters on the lines.

J

j

K

k

L

l

Tongue Twister Linda likes lemon lollipops.

Lesson 10: Mm, Nn, Oo

Write the letters on the lines.

Think and Link What other letters have round parts like the letter *O*?

Write the letters on the lines.

P

p

Q

q

R

r

Think and Link Say three animal names that begin like  .

Review

Look at the uppercase letter on each bunny. **Find** the carrot with each matching lowercase letter and **color** it to match the bunny's tail.

Riddle Time What dog can tell time?

Answer: A watch dog!

Lesson 13: Ss, Tt, Uu

Write the letters on the lines.

S s

T t

U u

Tongue Twister Sam sings silly songs.

I Can Do It!

Lesson 14: Vv, Ww, Xx

Write the letters on the lines.

V v

W w

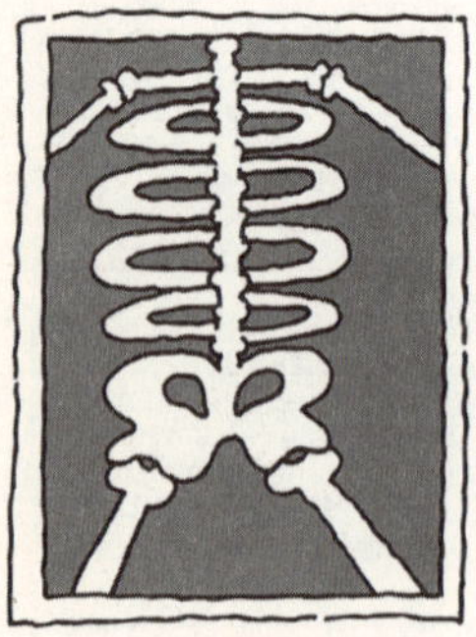

X x

Joke Corner Where do fish sleep?

Answer: In a water bed!

Lesson 15: Yy, Zz

I Can Do It!

Write the letters on the lines.

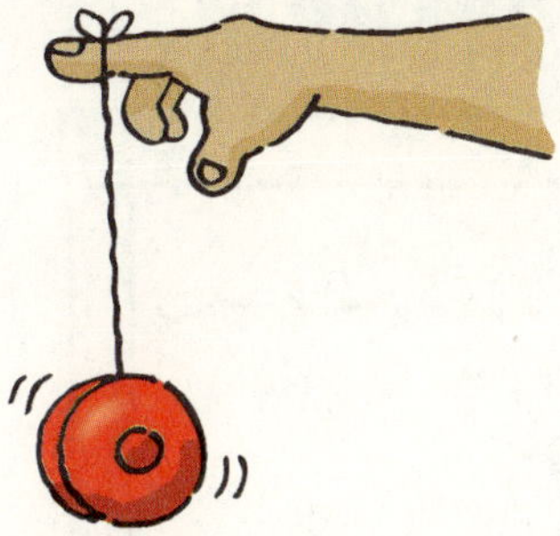

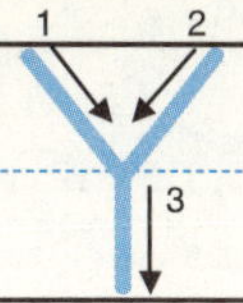

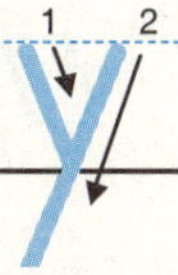

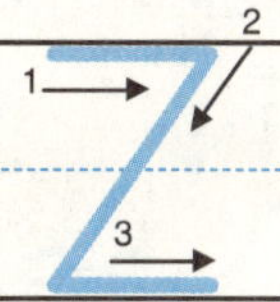

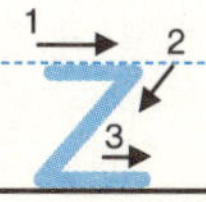

Look at the letters on each doghouse.
Circle each pair of uppercase and lowercase letters that match.

Review

Lesson 15: Review Uppercase and Lowercase Letters

Look at the letters on each fish.
Draw a line between each uppercase letter and its matching lowercase letter.

Read the poem.

Cat Kisses

by Bobbi Katz

Sandpaper kisses
on a cheek or a chin—
that is the way
for a day to begin!

Sandpaper kisses—
a cuddle, a purr.
I have an alarm clock
that's covered with fur.

Underline all of the uppercase matches for *s* in the poem.
Circle all of the lowercase matches for *I* in the poem.

Think and Link Name another type of pet. How would its kisses feel?

At Home Brainstorm pet words that start with the same letter as your child's name.

I Can Write It!

Lesson 17: Writing

Write your name on the line.
Draw a picture of yourself with a pet.

______________________'s Pet

Aa Bb Cc Dd Ee Ff Gg Hh Ii Jj Kk Ll Mm
Nn Oo Pp Qq Rr Ss Tt Uu Vv Ww Xx Yy Zz

Do you have a lot of pets too?
Sometimes it feels just like a zoo!

Too Many Pets

This book belongs to

____

My rabbit jumps out of his box.

My cat sleeps all night on my shirt.

My dog likes to roll in the dirt.

2

My fish swims between the rocks.

7

My guinea pig eats all day long.

4

My bird can sing silly songs.

5

In the Garden

Little Seeds

by Else Holmelund Minarik

Little seeds we sow in spring,
growing while the robins sing,
give us carrots, peas and beans,
tomatoes, pumpkins, squash and greens.

And we pick them,
one and all,
through the summer,
through the fall.

Winter comes, then spring, and then
little seeds we sow again.

On My Mind

What would you like to plant in a garden?

All-STARs at Home

Dear Family,

Our class is beginning Unit 2 of *SRA All-STAR Phonics*. Your child will be learning about consonant sounds while learning about the unit's theme, "In the Garden."

Here are some fun activities you can share with your child:

★ Turn over this letter. Read the poem "Little Seeds" by Else Holmelund Minarik with your child. Talk about how the seasons affect a garden. Together listen for the sound of *g* (as in *garden*) at the beginning, middle, and end of words. Say these words with your child and emphasize the /g/ sound.

★ Play a word game! Say a word, such as *bear*. Take turns with your child naming other words that begin with the same sound.

★ Sing silly songs! Choose a favorite song, such as "Happy Birthday." Change the first sound of each word to begin with the letter *t*, then sing the song together. "Tappy tirthday to tou…" This activity is sure to bring smiles as it helps your child develop an awareness of beginning sounds in words.

★ Look for books about gardens in the library or at the bookstore. We recommend:

- *Anna's Garden Songs* by Mary Q. Steele, Greenwillow Books, 1989.
- *Bumblebee, Bumblebee, Do You Know Me? A Garden Guessing Game* by Anne Rockwell, The Horn Book, Inc., 1999.

I Can Do It!

Say each picture name.
Color the pictures that begin like *dinosaur*.

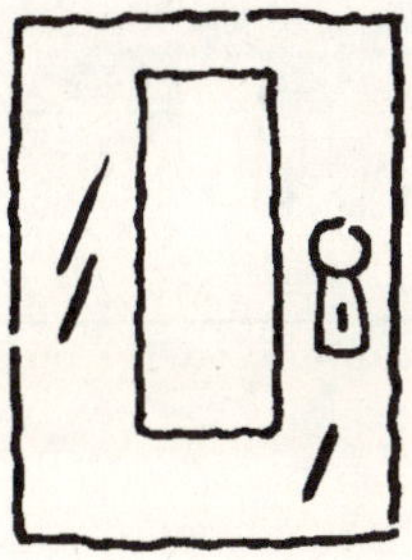

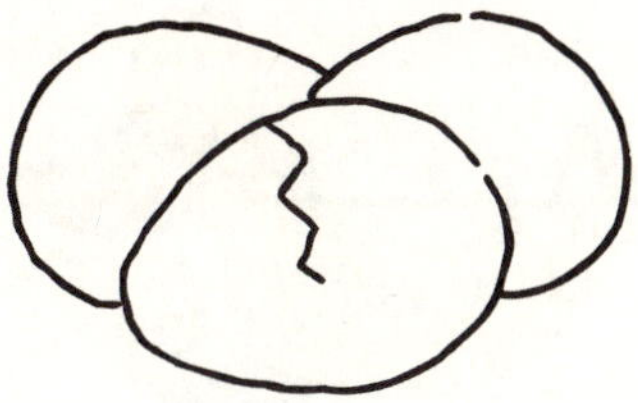

On-Track Fact The daisy was once called a "day's eye" because it is only open during the day. It closes at night.

I Can Do It!

Say each picture name. **Write** *d* on the line if the picture name begins like *dinosaur.*

1

d

2

3
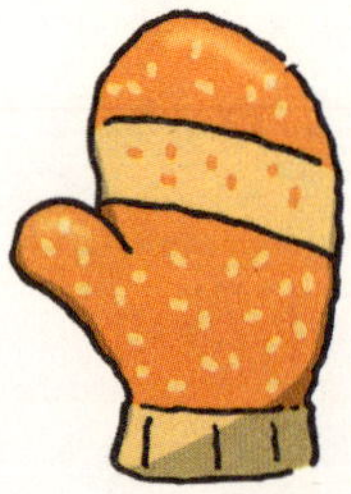

4

5

6

7

8

9

Tongue Twister Dig down the deep dark den.

I Can Do It!

Say each picture name.
Circle the pictures that begin like *monkey*.

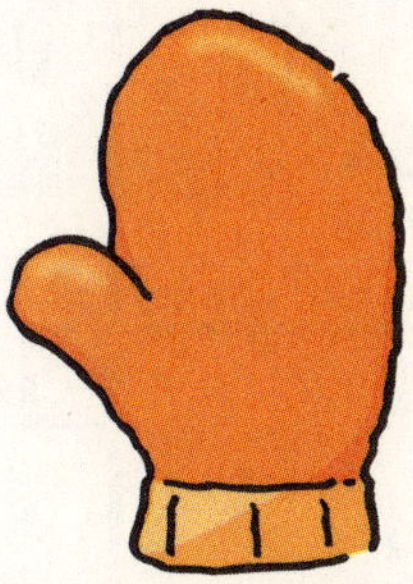

Riddle Time What room has no walls, no floor, and no ceiling?

A __ushroom!

I Can Do It!

Say each picture name.
Color each picture that begins like *monkey*.

Tongue Twister Milk makes much mush.

I Can Do It!

Say each picture name.
Circle the pictures that begin like *sun*.

Riddle Time What kind of fruit lives in a barn?

A _trawberry!

I Can Do It!

Say each picture name.
Write *s* under each picture that begins like *sun.*

1

s

2

3

4

5

6

7

8

9

Tongue Twister Swim, Sam, swim!

I Can Do It!

Say each picture name.
Draw a line from each *g* to a picture that begins like *girl*.

g g g g g g

Tongue Twister Green grapes and Greek grapes.

I Can Do It!

Lesson 4: Consonant Sounds: g

Say each picture name.
Write *g* on the line if the picture begins like *girl*.

1

g

2

3

4

5

6

7

8

9

Riddle Time What kind of flower is happiest?

A ___ladiola!

Lesson 5: Review Consonant Sounds: d, m, s, g

Review

Say each picture name. **Write** the letter that stands for the beginning sound. **Write** each word.

1

duck

duck

2

__ame

3

__oat

4

__esk

5

__ask

6

__ilk

Review

Say the sound that the letter stands for. **Color** the picture if it begins with the sound of the letter.

1 m

2 s

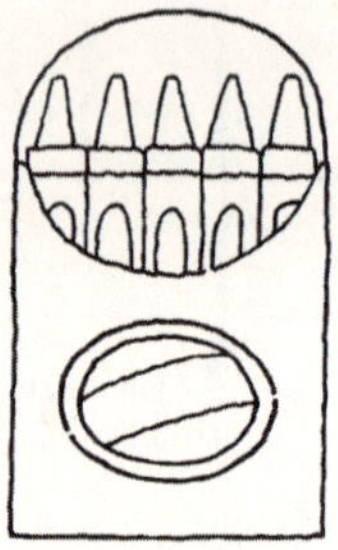

3 d

4 g

I Can Do It!

Say each picture name.
Fill in the circle under each picture that starts like *turtle.*

1

2
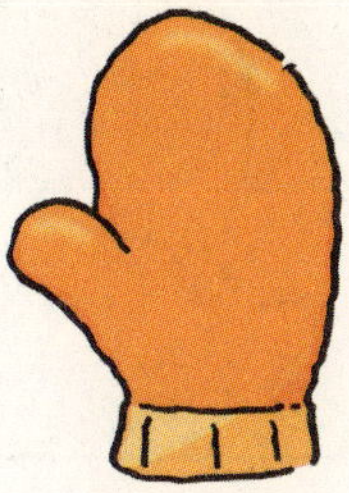

3
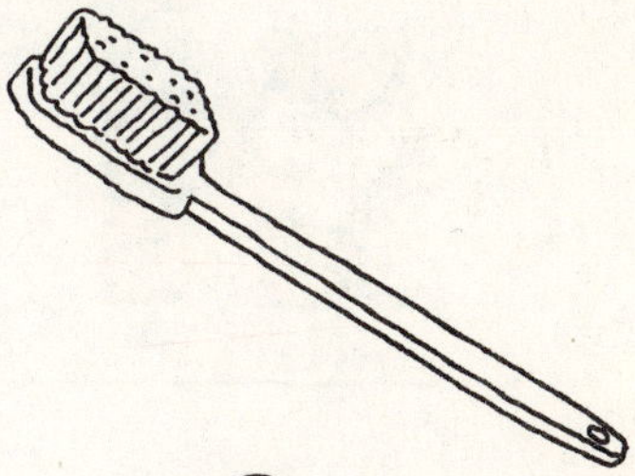

4

5

6

7
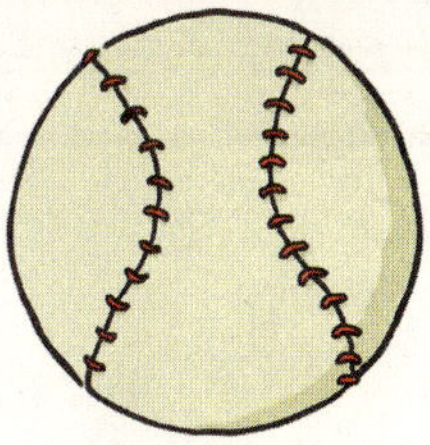

8

9
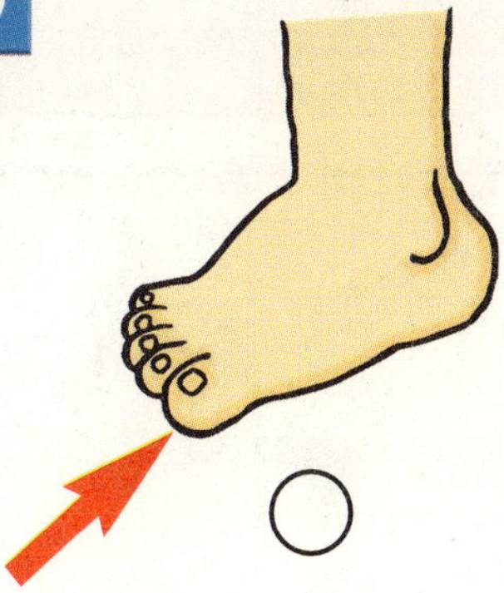

Riddle Time What flowers grow between your nose and your chin?

___ulips

I Can Do It!

Say each picture name.
Write *t* on the line if the picture begins like *turtle.*

1

t

2

3

4

5

6

7

8

9

Tongue Twister Toads have two toes too.

I Can Do It!

Say each picture name.
Fill in the circle under each picture that begins like *red*.

Tongue Twister Real rabbits run rapid races.

Lesson 7: Consonant Sounds: r

Say each picture name.
Write *r* on the line if the picture begins like *red*.

1

r

2

3

4

5

6

7

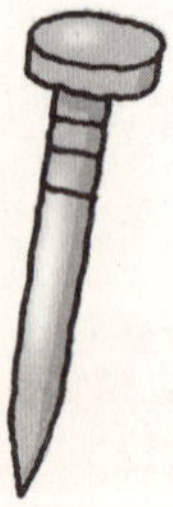

8

9

Say each picture name.
Color each picture that begins like *football.*

I Can Do It!

Lesson 8: Consonant Sounds: f

Trace each letter *f*. **Say** each picture name. **Draw** a line from *f* to the picture that begins like *football*.

1 f

2 f

3 f

4 f

5 f
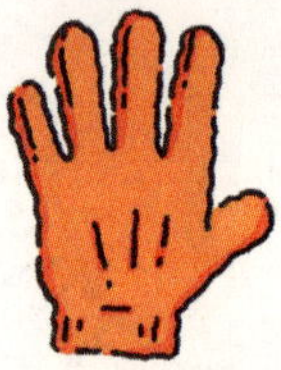
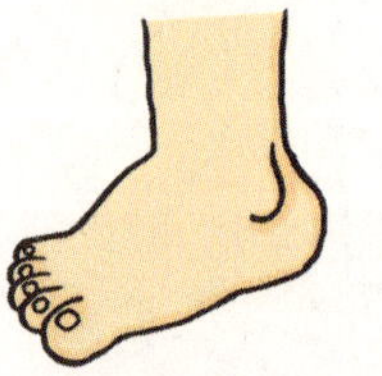

6 f

7 f

8 f

9 f
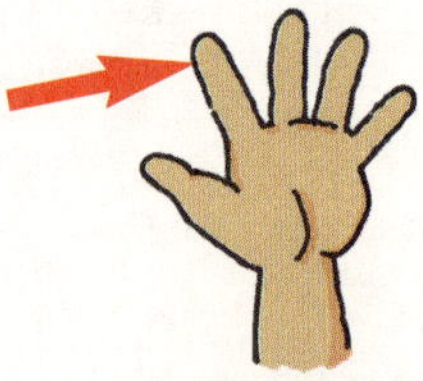

Tongue Twister Fred fries fresh fish.

Say each picture name.
Write *b* next to each picture that begins like *bike*. 

1

b

2

3

4

5

6

7

8

9

On-Track Fact Vanilla comes from a bean. 

I Can Do It!

Lesson 9: Consonant Sounds: b

Say each picture name. **Draw** an X on the pictures that do **not** begin like *bike*. 

Tongue Twister Betty bought better butter.

Review

Say the sound that the letter stands for.
Color the picture if it begins with the sound of the letter.

1 r

2 f

3 t

4 b

Big Idea Toads eat many insects.
Why would a toad be a good helper in a garden?

Review

Lesson 10: Review Consonant Sounds: t, r, f, b

Say each picture name. **Write** the letter that stands for the beginning sound. **Write** each word.

1

ring

ring

2

__an

3

__ox

4

__an

5

__ish

6

__abbit

I Can Do It!

Say each picture name. **Write** *n* under the pictures that begin like *nest.*

1

n

2

3

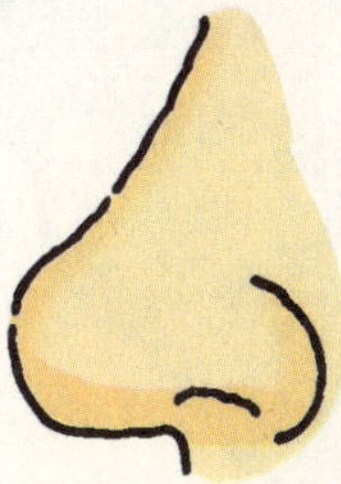

4

5

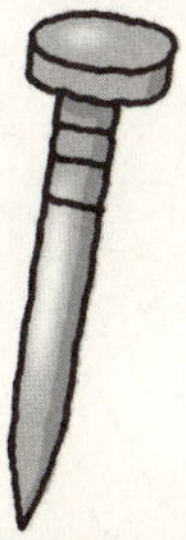

6

7

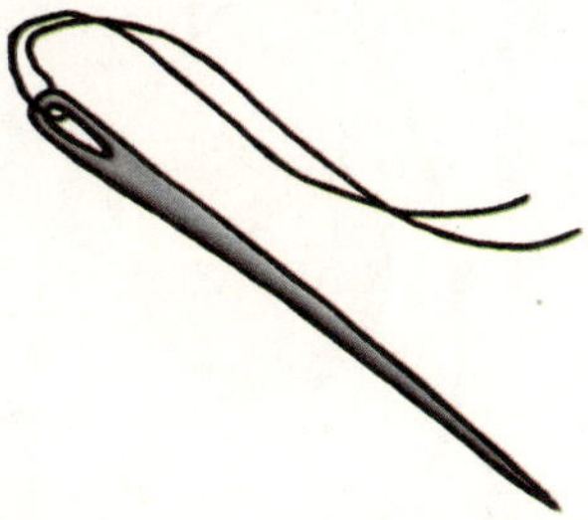

8

9

I Can Do It!

Say each picture name. Draw an X on the egg if the picture does **not** begin like *nest*.

Tongue Twister Nine nice newts eat new noodles.

I Can Do It!

Say each picture name.
Circle the pictures that begin like *kite*.

Tongue Twister Crazy kite kits.

I Can Do It!

Lesson 12: Consonant Sounds: k

Say each picture name. **Draw** a line from each raindrop with a *k* to a picture that begins like *kite*.

I Can Do It!

Say each picture name.
Fill in the circle under each picture that begins like *pencil.*

1

2

3

4

5

6

7
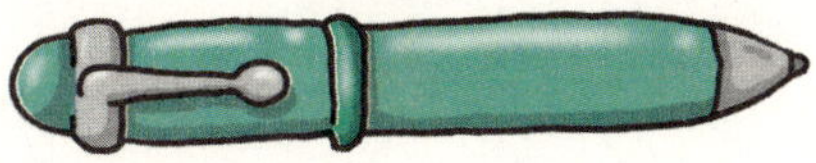

8

9

Think and Link Name all the things you can find in a garden that begin with the letter *p.*

I Can Do It!

Lesson 13: Consonant Sounds: p

Say each picture name.
Write *p* beside each picture that begins like *pencil.*

1

p

2
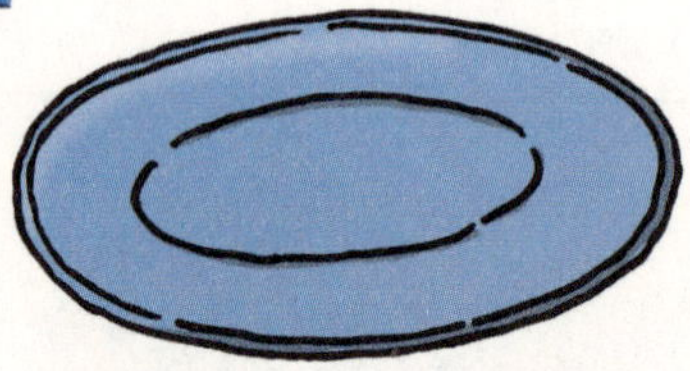

3

4

5

6

7

8

9

Tongue Twister Peter Piper picked a peck of pickled peppers.

I Can Do It!

Trace each letter *l*. Say each picture name.
Draw a line from the letter *l* to the picture that begins like *lamp*. 

Big Idea Did you know that spinach is the leaf of the plant? What other plant leaves do you eat for food?

I Can Do It!

Lesson 14: Consonant Sounds: l

Say each picture name.
Color each picture that begins like *lamp.*

1

2

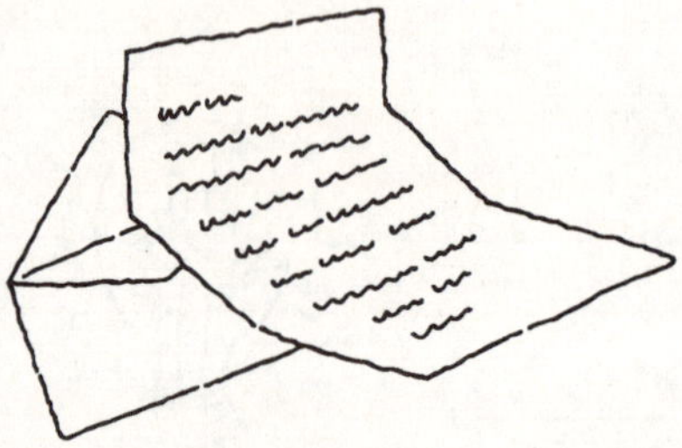

3

4

5

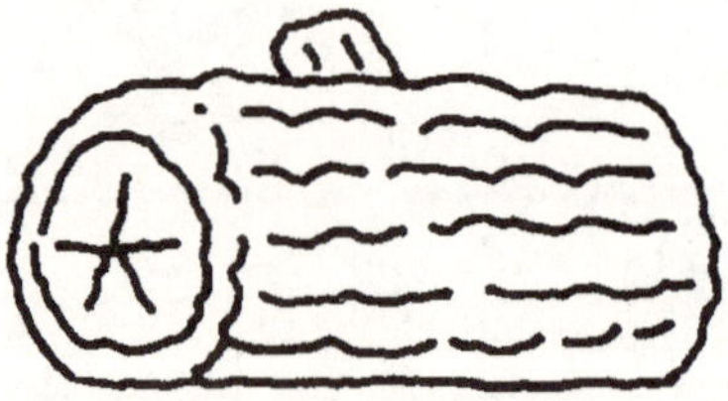

6

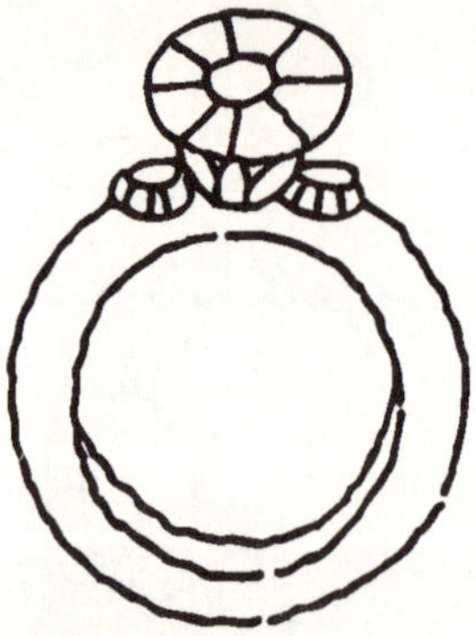

7

8

9

Tongue Twister Larry lost the last letter.

Review

Trace each letter. **Say** the sound that the letter stands for.
Color the picture if it begins with the sound of the letter.

1

n

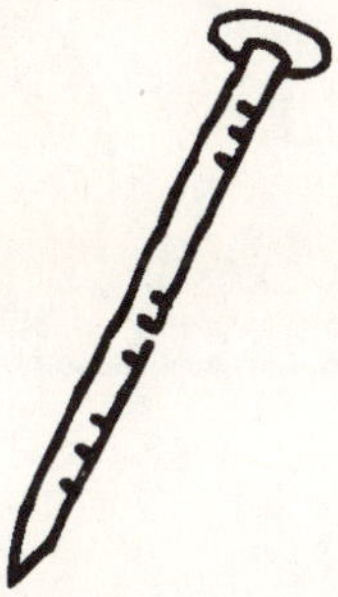

2

k

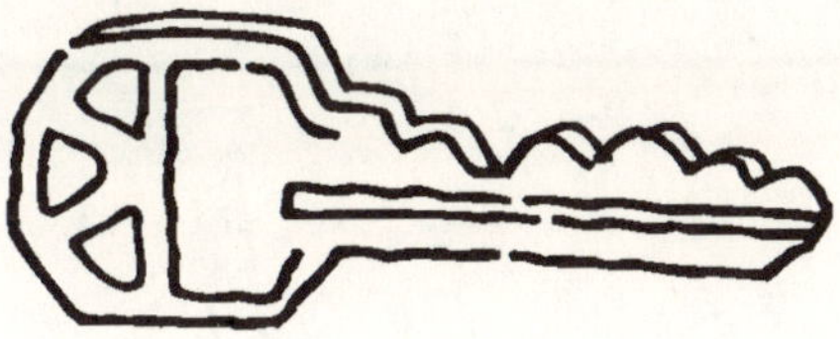

3

l

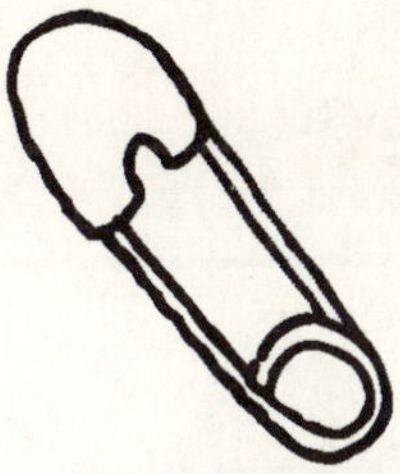

4

p

On-Track Fact Plants give us food.
They help clean the air too!

Review

Lesson 15: Review Consonant Sounds: n, k, p, l

Say the name of the pictures in each row. **Write** the letter that stands for the beginning sound of the pictures in each row.

1

_____

2

_____

3

_____

4

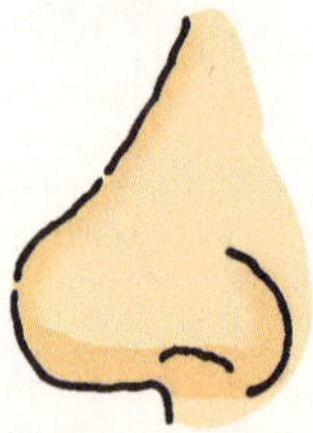
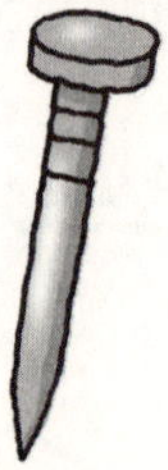

_____

Rhyme Time Listen for the rhyming words.

Mary Mary quite contrary,
How does your garden grow?
With silver bells and cockle-shells,
And silver maids all in a row.

I Can Do It!

Write the letter *h* on each line.
Say each picture name. **Draw** a line from the letter *h* to a picture that begins like *horse*. 

h

Tongue Twister Hurry, Heidi! Help Harry!

I Can Do It!

Lesson 16: Consonant Sounds: h

Say each picture name. **Draw** an X on the pictures that do **not** begin like *horse.* 

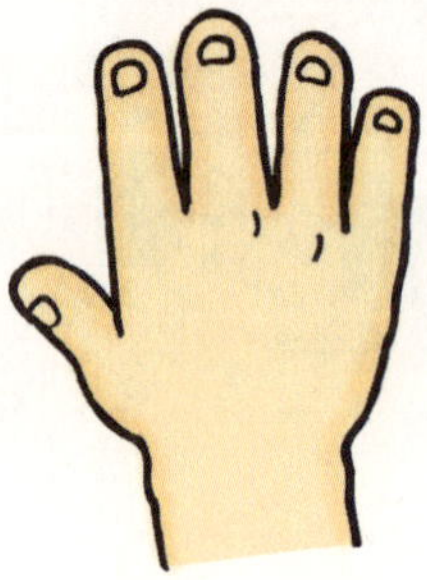

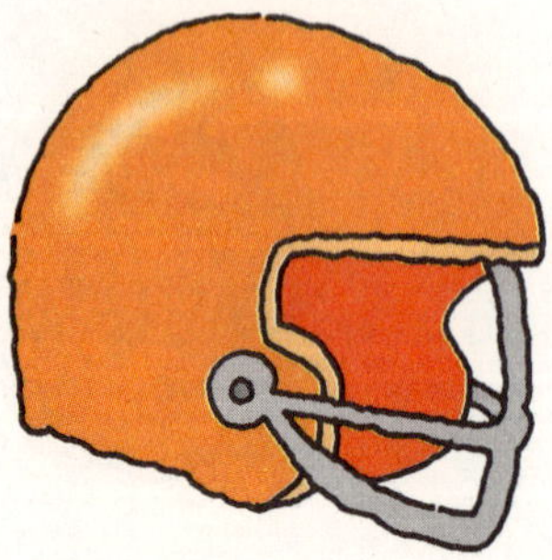

I Can Do It!

Write the letter *j* on each line.
Say each picture name. Draw a line from the letter *j* to the picture that begins like *jump*. 

1

j

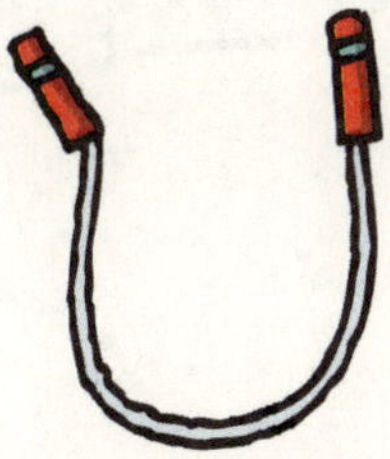

3

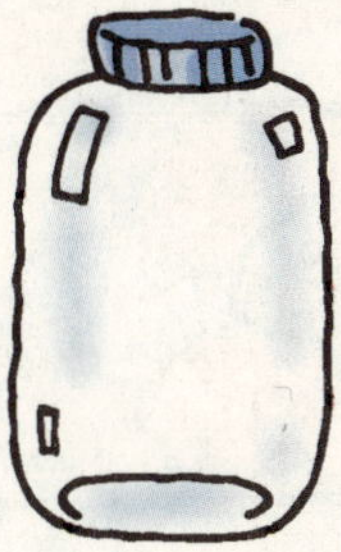

2

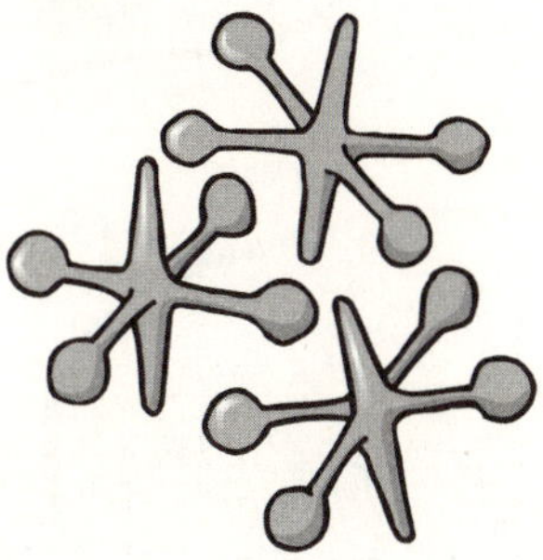

4

Big Idea Oranges give us vitamin C, which our bodies need. What other foods give us vitamin C?

I Can Do It!

Say each picture name. Color the jellybeans that have a picture that begins like *jump*.

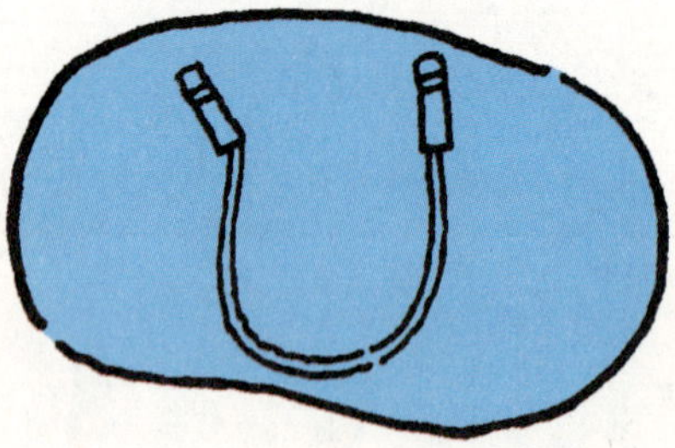

Tongue Twister Joe's jelly jiggles.

Lesson 18: Consonant Sounds: w

I Can Do It!

Say each picture name. **Draw** a line from the *w* in the middle to the pictures that begin like *watch*.

Tongue Twister How much wood would a woodchuck chuck if a woodchuck could chuck wood?

I Can Do It!

Lesson 18: Consonant Sounds: w

Say each picture name.
Color the pictures that begin like *watch*.

Say each picture name.
Circle the pictures that begin like *car*. 

Joke Corner

Knock, knock!
Who's there?
Rosa!
Rosa who?
Rosa carrots grow in the garden!

I Can Do It!

Say each picture name.
Color each picture that begins like *car*. 

1 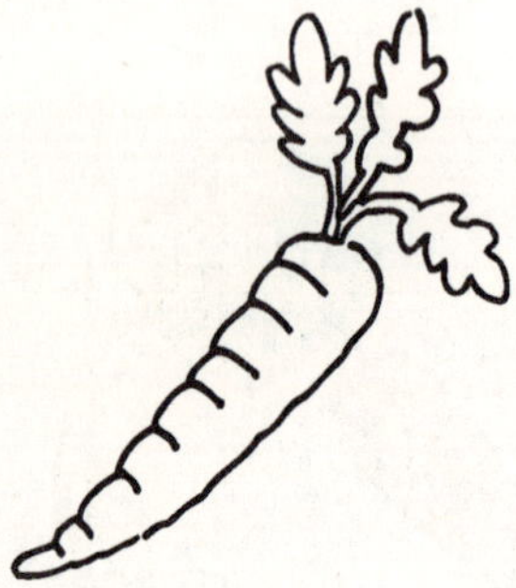

2 

3 

4 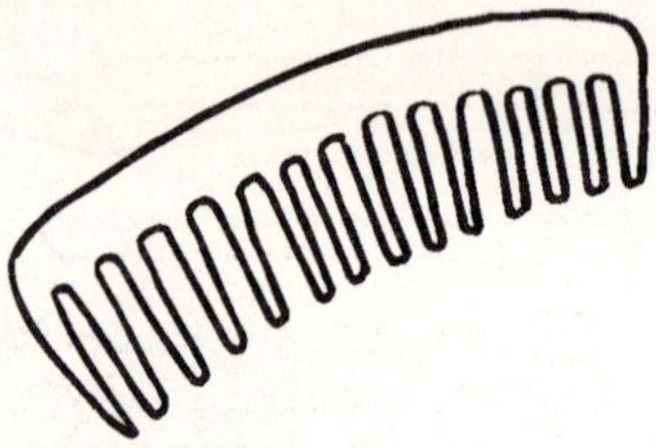

5 

6 

7 

8 

9 

10 

11 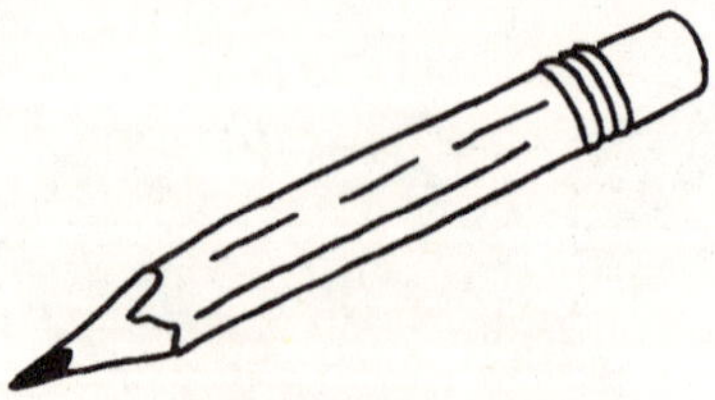

12 

Tongue Twister Clams can come in cans.

Review

Trace the letter. **Say** each picture name.
Color the pictures that begin with the sound of the letter.

1

j

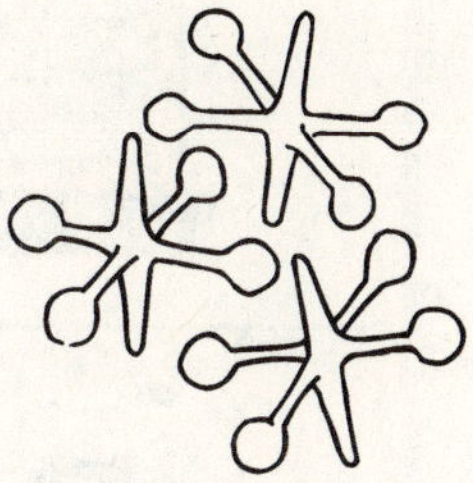

2

c

3

w

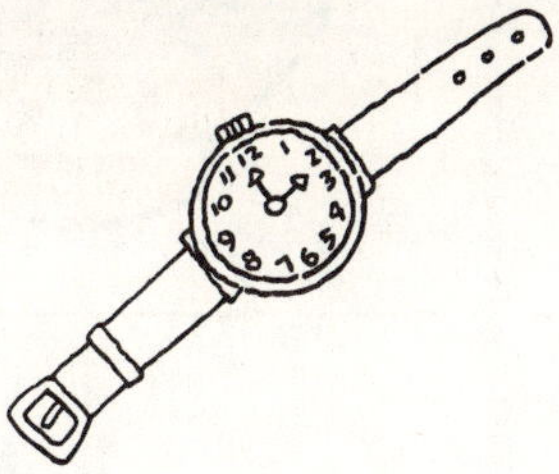

4

h

Review

Say each picture name. Write the letter that stands for the beginning sound. Write each word.

1

cookies
cookies

2

___indow

3
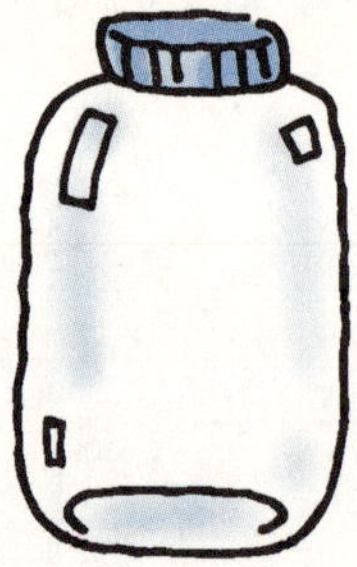
___ar

4

___ig

5

___up

6

___ouse

Joke Corner How do you tell which end of the worm is the head?

Answer: Tickle the middle and see which end laughs!

Say each picture name. **Draw** a line from the letter *v* to the picture that begins like *van.* 

1

v

2

v

3

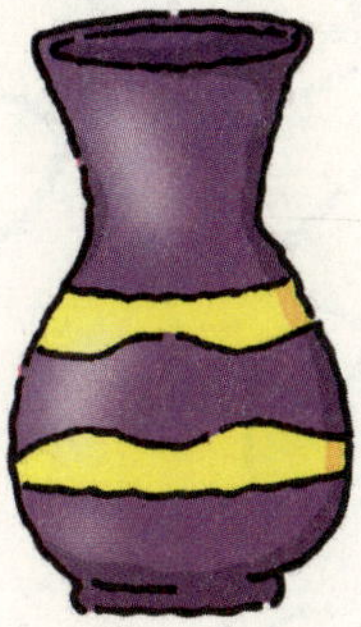

v

4

v

On-Track Fact Worms are good for a garden. They keep the soil loose. They also make food for the plants.

I Can Do It!

Say each picture name.
Color the stem of each flower that has a picture that begins like *van.* 

Tongue Twister Vets drive vans.

I Can Do It!

Write the letter *y* on each line.
Say each picture name. Draw a line from the letter *y* to a picture that begins like *yo-yo*.

y

y

y

y

Tongue Twister Yaks yank yellow yo-yos.

I Can Do It!

Lesson 22: Consonant Sounds: y

Say each picture name.
Color the picture yellow if it begins like *yo-yo*.

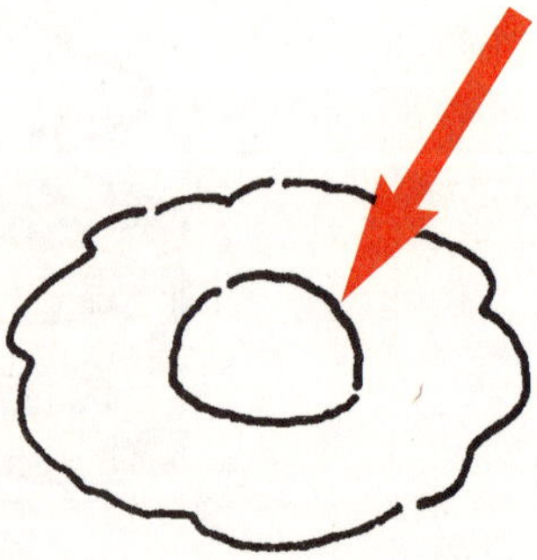

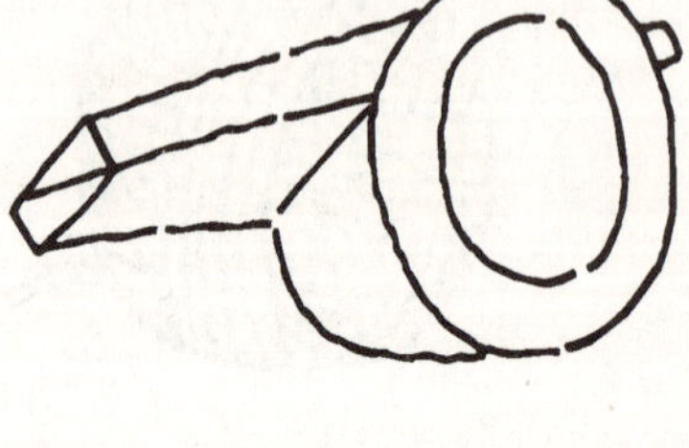

I Can Do It!

Trace each letter *q*. **Say** each picture name. **Circle** the picture that begins like *queen*.

1 q

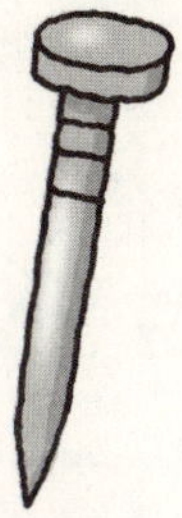
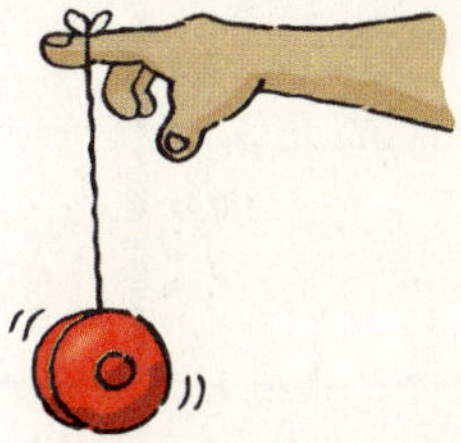

2 q

3 q

4 q

All-STAR Extra The letter *q* is the only letter of the alphabet that does not appear in the name of any state in the United States.

I Can Do It!

Lesson 24: Consonant Sounds: x

The sound of *x* is at the **end** of words.
Trace each *x*. Say each picture name.
Circle the pictures that **end** like *fox*.

1 x

2 x

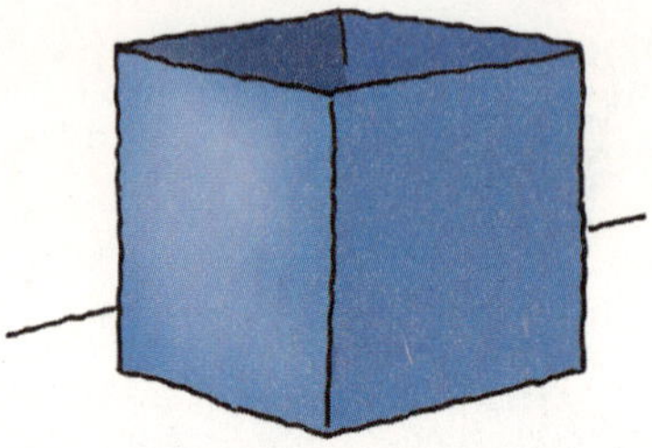

3 x

4 x

Tongue Twister Six foxes in trick boxes.

I Can Do It!

Say each picture name.
Fill in the circle near each picture that begins like *zebra.* 
Connect the dots to make a letter.

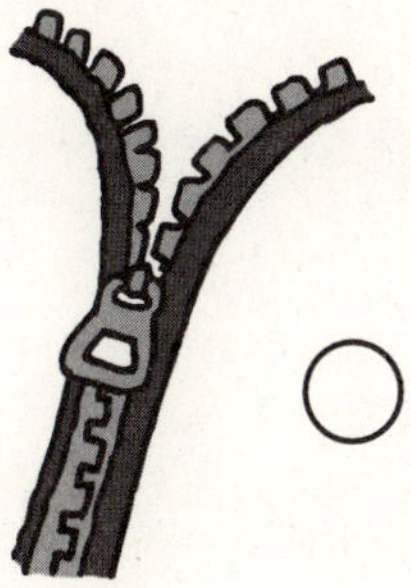

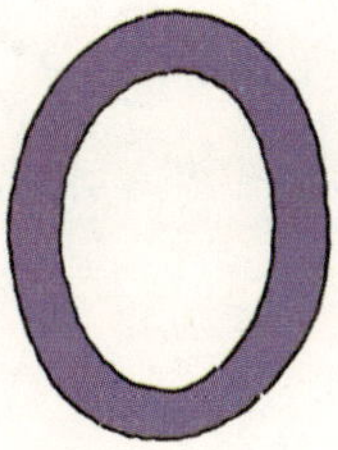

Think and Link Where can you see a zebra?

At the _oo.

I Can Do It!

Say each picture name. **Draw** a line from each letter z to a picture that begins like *zebra.*

z

z

z

z

On-Track Fact Did you know that squirrels plant trees? Sometimes they bury their nuts and forget to dig them up. The buried nuts grow into trees.

Review

Say each picture name. **Draw** a line from each letter to the picture that begins with the letter sound.

v

y

q

z

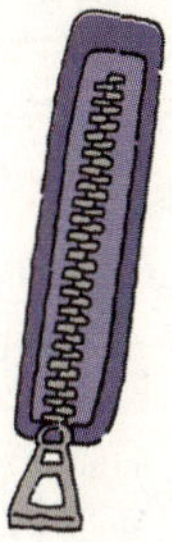

Tongue Twister Quietly ask quick questions.

Review

Lesson 26: Review Consonant Sounds: v, y, q, x, z

Trace the letter. **Say** the name of each picture. **Color** the picture that begins with the sound of the letter.

1 y

2 z

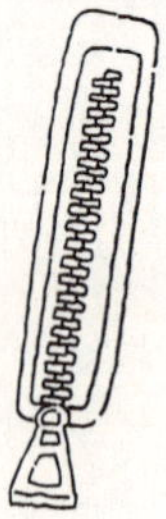

3 v

Trace the letter. **Say** the name of each picture. **Color** the picture that ends like *fox*. 

4 x

5 x

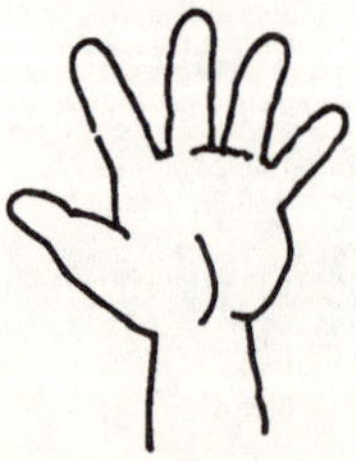

I Can Read It!

Seed, Sprout, Flower

by Helen H. Moore

A seed is planted:
First a sprout,
then stem,
and leaves,
and buds
come out.
Buds grow bigger,
smelling sweet,
bees and birds come
'round to eat.
Bees and birds
help flowers spread
their new seeds on
the garden bed . . .
A seed is planted.

Circle the words that begin with the letter *b*.
Draw a box around each word that begins with the letter *s*.

At Home Read the poem "Seed, Sprout, Flower" together. Look for words that have the same beginning sounds, such as *first* and *flowers.* Ask your child to say as many words as he or she can think of that begin with that consonant sound.

I Can Write It!

Lesson 28: Writing

Say each picture name. Write the letter that stands for the sound you hear at the beginning of the word.

1

3

2

4

Draw your garden. Write the letter that stands for the beginning sound of three things in your garden.

The Surprise Seed

This book belongs to ______________________

1

Will it be a flower or vegetable?
Let's see.

3

Then I find a sunny window.

6

Surprise! A red flower for me.

8

My teacher gave me a seed.

2

I will not forget to water it!

7

I put dirt in a yellow pot.

4

Now I push the seed down and cover it.

5

Can I Help?

Good-Bye Six, Hello Seven

by Judith Viorst

I'm getting a higher bunk bed.
And I'm getting a bigger bike.
And I'm getting to cross Connecticut Avenue
all by myself, if I like.
And I'm getting to help do dishes.
And I'm getting to weed the yard.
And I'm getting to think that seven
could be hard.

On My Mind

How do you help at home?
How will you help when you are older?

All-STARs at Home

Dear Family,

Our class is beginning Unit 3 of *SRA All-STAR Phonics*. Your child will be learning to recognize short vowel sounds while learning about the theme "Can I Help?" These vowel sounds help your child to begin to blend, or "sound out," simple, three-letter words. Your child will soon be well on his or her way to reading! The following examples show words with short vowel sounds:

a in **cat** ***e*** in **pet** ***i*** in **pig** ***o*** in **hot** ***u*** in **tub**

Here are some fun activities your child can help to do:

★ Turn over this letter. Together read with your child the poem "Good-Bye Six, Hello Seven" by Judith Viorst. Talk about the different ways that children can help as they get older. Discuss ways that your child helps at home.

★ **Ticcolo Taccolo Too** Say the following rhyme several times until your child can say it with you:

Ticcolo taccolo too,
A kitty is by you!
Ticcolo taccolo tee,
A puppy is by me!

Repeat the rhyme, changing the last word of the first line to rhyme with the name of a family member, such as *Ticcolo taccolo taddy*. Then finish the rhyme, having your child supply the family member's name for the last word: *A kitty is by Daddy.*

★ Look for books about helpers in the library or at the bookstore. We recommend:

- *Have You Seen My Cat?* by Eric Carle, Aladdin Paperbacks, 1997.
- *The Little Red Hen: An Old Story* by Margot Zemach, Sunburst, 1993.

All-STAR Readers Know

The letter *a* is a vowel. It can stand for the short sound you hear at the beginning of the word *apple*. 

Say each picture name. **Listen** for the short sound of *a*. **Draw** a line from the apple to each picture that has the short sound of *a*.

Big Idea Why is helping important?

Lesson 1: Introducing Short *a* Sound /ă/

Say each picture name. **Listen** for the short sound of *a*. **Circle** each picture that has the short sound of *a*.

1

2

3

4

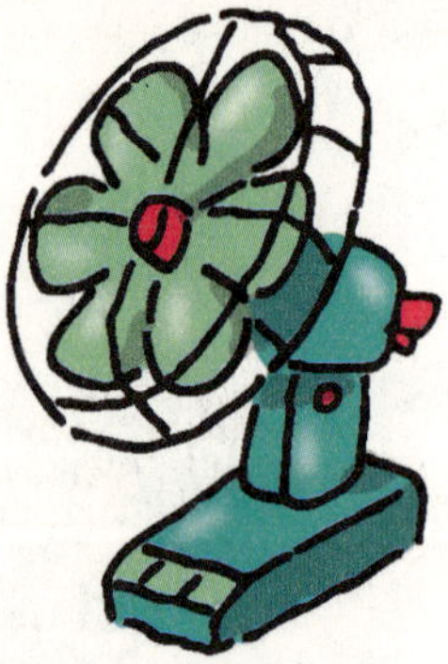

5

6

7

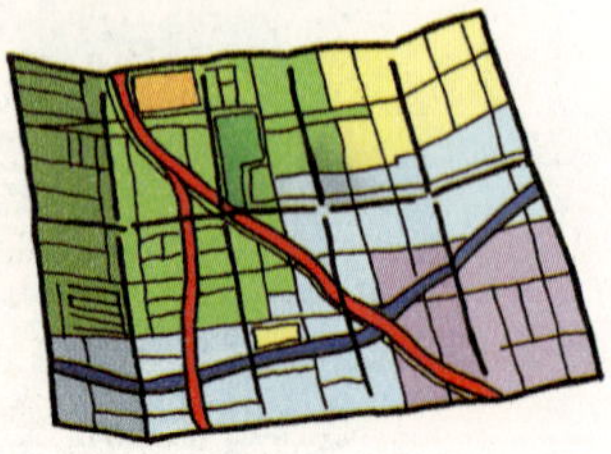

8

9

Think and Link Who are helpers at your school?

I Can Do It!

Say each picture name. Listen for the short sound of *a*. Write *a* under each picture that has the short sound of *a*.

1

a

2

3

4
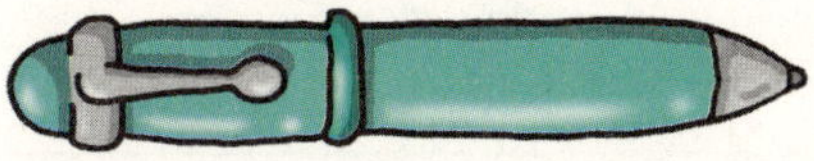

5
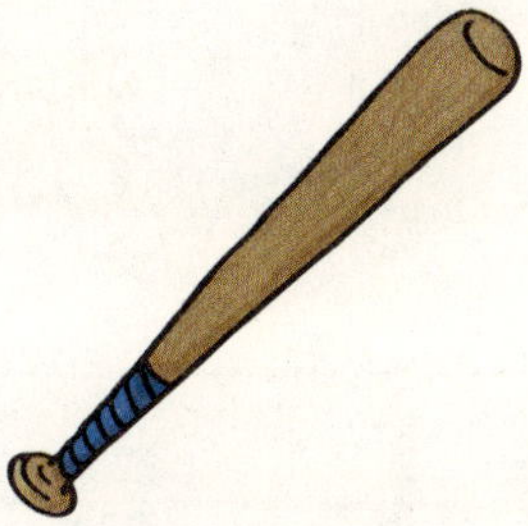

6

7
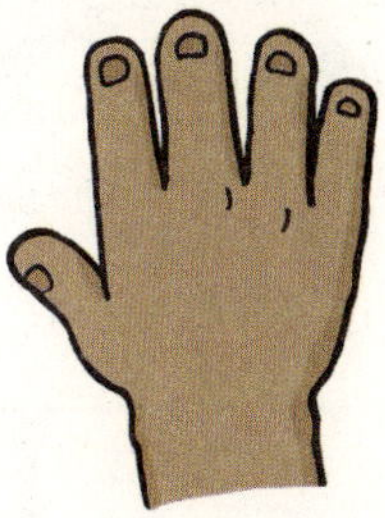

8

9

I Can Do It!

Lesson 2: Identifying Short *a* Sound /ă/

Say each picture name. **Listen** for the short sound of *a*. **Write** *a* on the line to complete the word if the picture name has the short sound of *a*.

1 

c a t

2 

v ___ n

3 

p ___ g

4 

m ___ n

5 

b ___ x

6 

b ___ t

7 

f ___ n

8 

c ___ p

9 

s ___ d

Tongue Twister Tap, clap, tap, clap.

I Can Do It!

Say each letter sound. Blend the sounds to read the word. Draw a line to match the picture to the word that names the picture.

1

f a n c a n

4

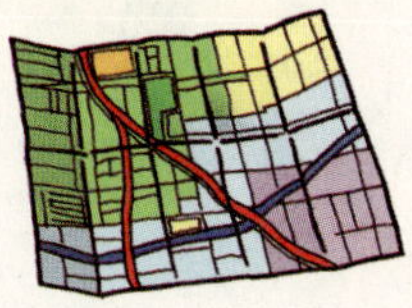

m a p c a p

2

h a t c a t

5

s a d m a d

3

p a n m a n

6

b a g r a g

On-Track Fact Some dogs help people. How do dogs help?

I Can Do It!

Lesson 3: Blending Short *a* Sound /ă/

Say each picture name. Listen to the sounds of the letters as they blend together. Write the picture name on the line.

1 

? a d

sad

2 

? a t

3 

? a n

4 

? a m

5 

? a t

6 

? a p

I Can Do It!

Say each picture name. **Listen** for the short sound of *a*.
Write the picture name on the line.

1

hat

2

3

4
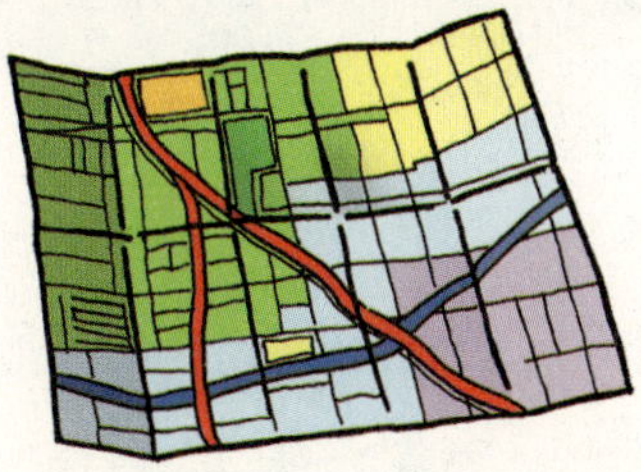

5

6

7

8

9

Tongue Twister Ann saw ants in Aunt Annie's attic.

I Can Do It!

Lesson 4: Writing and Reading Short a Sound /ă/

Say each picture name. **Listen** for the short sound of *a*. **Fill in** the circle in front of the word that names the picture.

1

● cap ○ can

2

○ sat ○ sad

3

○ fat ○ fan

4

○ man ○ map

5

○ pat ○ pan

6

○ hat ○ ham

7

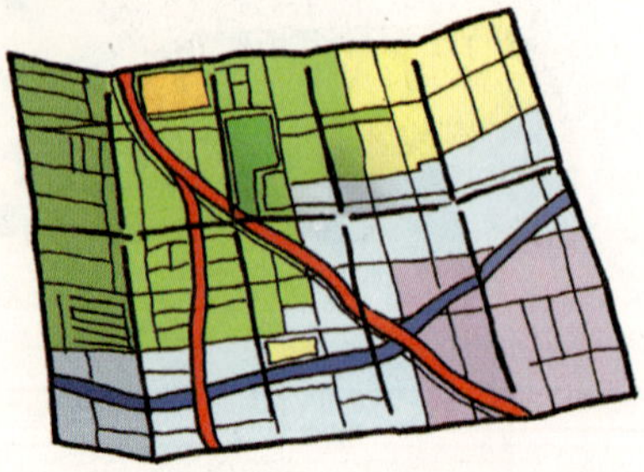

○ map ○ mat

8

○ nap ○ pan

9

○ mat ○ mad

I Can Do It!

Say each picture name. **Listen** for names that rhyme. **Draw** a line to match the rhyming pictures.

Big Idea What can you do to help at home?

I Can Do It!

Lesson 5: Rhyming Words with Short *a* Sound /ă/

Say each picture name. **Circle** the rhyming pictures. **Write** the rhyming words on the lines.

1

 cat  hat

 can  mad

cat

hat

2

 lap  can

 sad  man

3

 rag  bat

 bag  jam

Joke Corner What do you call a big kitty?

A f__t c__t!

Read each sentence. **Fill in** the circle next to the word that makes sense in the sentence. **Write** the word on the line.

1. The  has a cat.
   - ○ bad
   - ● cat
   - ○ mad

2. Dan has a ______ .
   - ○ rat
   - ○ ran
   - ○ tan

3. Max ______ to the .
   - ○ ran
   - ○ sat
   - ○ man

4. Pam ______ on a 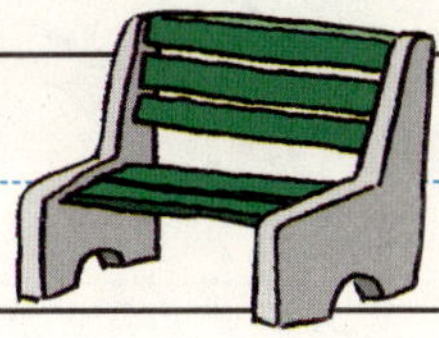.
   - ○ mat
   - ○ sat
   - ○ hat

5. Ann can  the ______.
   - ○ sat
   - ○ van
   - ○ bad

6. The  had a ______.
   - ○ nap
   - ○ sat
   - ○ sad

I Can Do It!

Lesson 6: Using Short *a* Sound /ă/ in Context

Read each sentence.
Write the sentence that tells about the picture.

1

Dan has a hat.
Dan has a ham.

Dan has a hat.

2

The cat naps on a mat.
The cat naps on a lap.

3

Jan has a pan.
Jan has a bat.

4

Pam sat on the cab.
Dad sat in the van.

I Can Do It!

All-STAR Readers Know

The letter *i* is a vowel. It can stand for the short sound you hear at the beginning of the word *igloo.* 

Say each picture name. **Listen** for the short sound of *i*. **Draw** a line from the igloo to each picture that has the short sound of *i*.

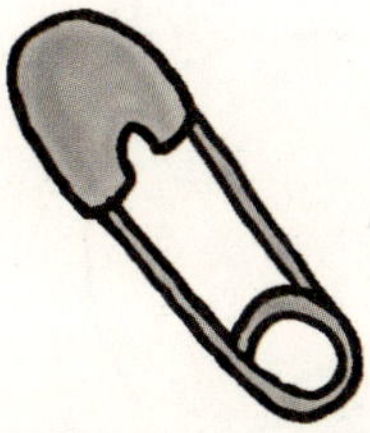

Think and Link What can you do to help your grandparents?

I Can Do It!

Lesson 7: Introducing Short *i* Sound /ĭ/

Say each picture name. **Listen** for the short sound of *i*. **Color** each picture that has the short sound of *i*.

1

2
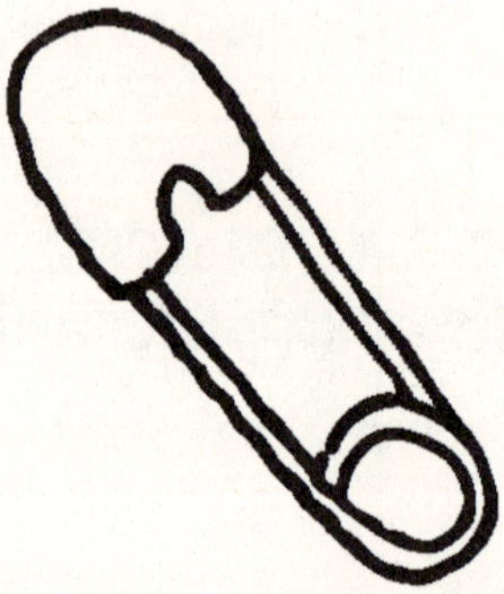

3
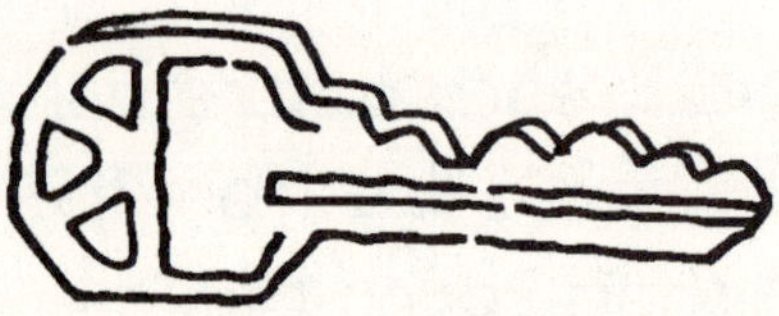

4

5

6

7

8

9
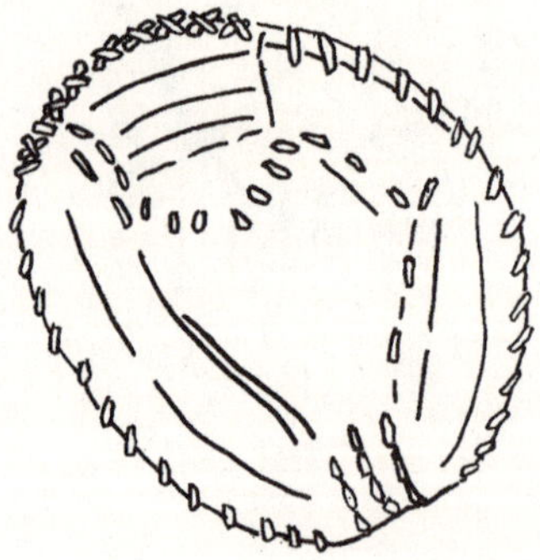

Lesson 8: Identifying Short *i* Sound /ĭ/

I Can Do It!

Say each picture name. **Listen** for the short sound of *i*.
Write *i* under each picture that has the short sound of *i*.

1

i

2

3

4

5

6

7

8

9

I Can Do It!

Lesson 8: Identifying Short *i* Sound /ĭ/

Say each picture name. **Listen** for the short sound of *i*. **Write** *i* on the line to complete the word if the picture name has the short sound of *i*.

1

p i n

2

h _ t

3

p _ g

4

z _ p

5

m _ n

6

f _ n

7

w _ g

8

j _ t

9

d _ g

I Can Do It!

Say each letter sound. **Blend** the sounds to read the word. **Draw** a line to match the picture to the word that names the picture.

1

sit pit

4

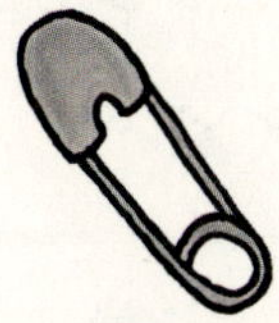

pin fin

2

wig pig

5

lip rip

3

mix six

6

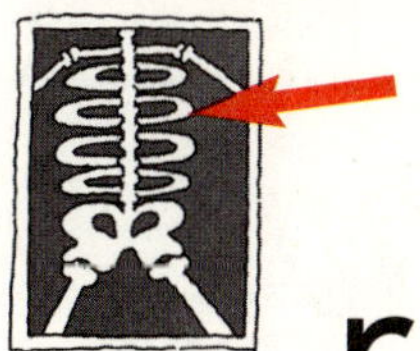

bib rib

Big Idea Why do people sometimes need help?

I Can Do It!

Lesson 9: Blending Short *i* Sound /ĭ/

Say each picture name. **Listen** to the sounds of the letters as they blend together. **Write** the picture name on the line.

1 

? i t

hit

2 

? i g

3 

? i n

4 

? i g

5 

? i t

Think and Link Which of these are *helping* words? Why?

give **lift** **sip** **pig**

I Can Do It!

Say each picture name. **Listen** for the short sound of *i*. **Write** the picture name on the line.

1

fin

2

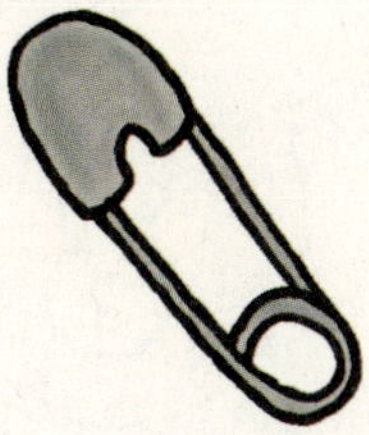

3

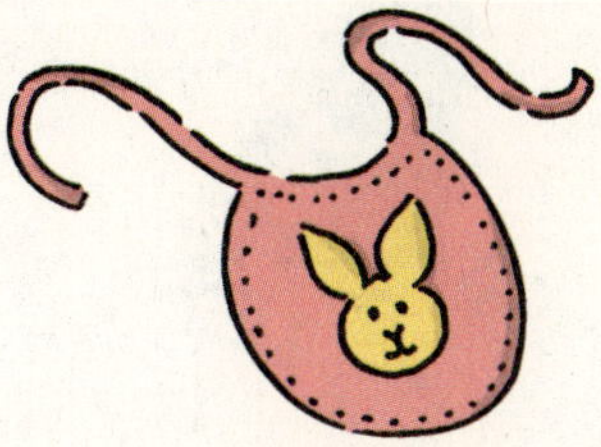

4

5

6

7

8

9

I Can Do It!

Lesson 10: Writing and Reading Short *i* Sound /ĭ/

Say each picture name. **Listen** for the short sound of *i*. **Fill in** the circle in front of the word that names the picture.

1

● fin ○ fit

2

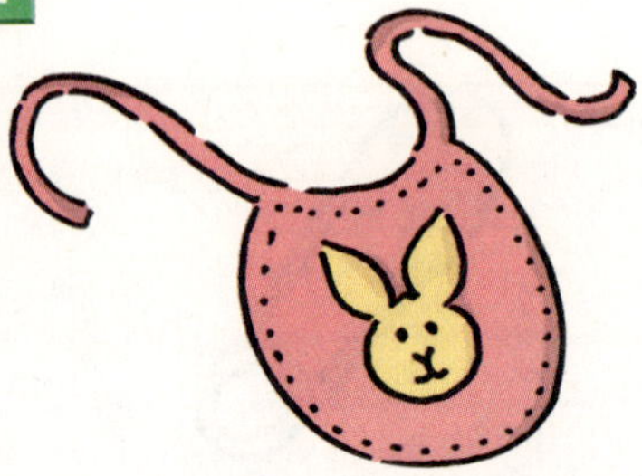

○ bib ○ big

3

○ pig ○ wig

4

○ rip ○ rib

5

○ pin ○ pit

6

○ mix ○ six

7

○ sit ○ sip

8

○ lid ○ lip

9

○ dip ○ dig

Think and Link If you pick up litter, how would you be helping your community?

Say each picture name. **Listen** for names that rhyme. **Draw** a line to match the rhyming pictures.

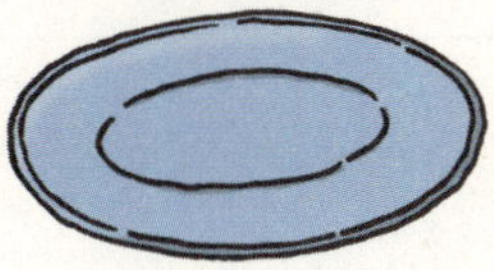

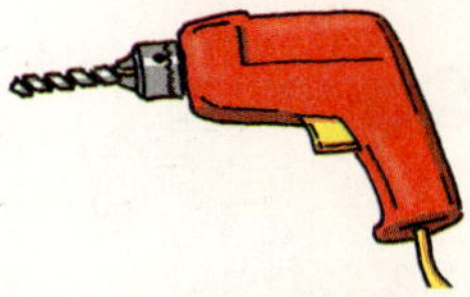

Rhyme Time

Jack and Jill
Went up the hill
To fetch a pail of water.
Jack fell down
And broke his crown
And Jill came tumbling after.

I Can Do It!

Lesson 11: Rhyming Words with Short *i* Sound /ĭ/

Say each picture name. **Circle** the rhyming pictures. **Write** the rhyming words on the lines.

1

 sit  hat — sit

 hit  fish — hit

2

 pin  fin

 pan  lip

3

 pit  pig

 wig  dig

Joke Corner What is hair for a hog?

A p___g w___g!

I Can Do It!

Read each sentence. **Fill in** the circle next to the word that makes sense in the sentence. **Write** the word on the line.

1. Kim hit six 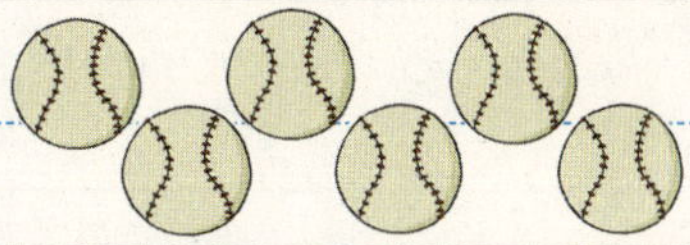.
   - ● hit
   - ○ sit
   - ○ hip

2. The  did not ____.
   - ○ bit
   - ○ fit
   - ○ lid

3. Did Tim ____ the ?
   - ○ wig
   - ○ fin
   - ○ win

4. Lin will ____ in the .
   - ○ dig
   - ○ fin
   - ○ sit

5. Dad will ____ the 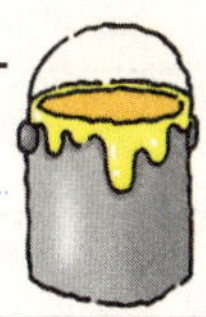.
   - ○ mix
   - ○ pin
   - ○ lip

6. The  can ____.
   - ○ dig
   - ○ big
   - ○ rip

I Can Do It!

Lesson 12: Using Short *i* Sound /ĭ/ in Context

Read each sentence. Write the sentence that tells about the picture.

1

Cap is a big pig.
Cap is a big pin.

Cap is a big pig.

2

Tim can fix a pin.
Tim can dig a pit.

3

Pat fits in.
Pat sits down.

4

Did Max pin it?
Did Max miss it?

Review

Read each set of words below. Combine words from each set to write three complete sentences.

1

2

3

On-Track Fact Children all over the country help others on National Youth Service Day. What are some ways your class might help others?

Review

Lesson 13: Review Short *a, i* Sounds /ă/, /ĭ/

Look at each picture. **Read** the words in the box. **Write** a sentence about each picture. Use the words in the box to help you.

cap	man	dig	pig	sad	has	sit

1

2

All-STAR Readers Know

The letter *o* is a vowel. It can stand for the short sound you hear at the beginning of the word *octopus*. 

Say each picture name. **Listen** for the short sound of *o*. **Circle** each picture that has the short sound of *o*.

Tongue Twister Pop's popcorn popper pops Pop's popcorn.

I Can Do It!

Lesson 14: Introducing Short *o* Sound /ŏ/

Look for things that have the short sound of *o*. **Circle** five things whose names have the short sound of *o*.

Lesson 15: Identifying Short *o* Sound /ŏ/

I Can Do It!

Say each picture name. **Listen** for the short sound of *o*.
Write *o* under each picture that has the short sound of *o*.

1

o

2

3
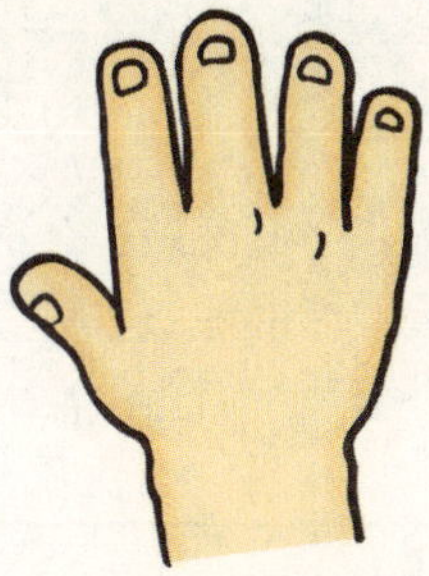

4

5

6

7

8

9

Big Idea What do you need help with sometimes?

I Can Do It!

Lesson 15: Identifying Short *o* Sound /ŏ/

Say each picture name. **Listen** for the short sound of *o*. **Write** *o* on the line to complete the word if that picture name has the short sound of *o*.

1  b o x	2  f ___ x	3  c ___ t
4  p ___ g	5  p ___ t	6  h ___ t
7  c ___ p	8  p ___ p	9  c ___ b

I Can Do It!

Say each letter sound. **Blend** the sounds to read the word. **Draw** a line to match the picture to the word that names the picture.

1

top mop

4

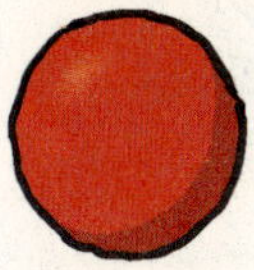

dot hot

2

dog log

5

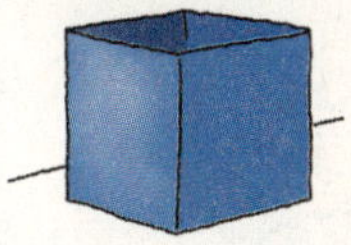

box fox

3

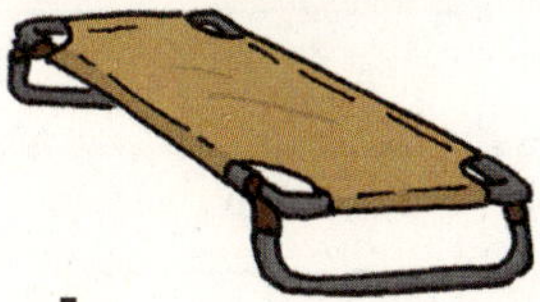

cot pot

6

Bob cob

Think and Link How can you thank someone who helps you?

I Can Do It!

Lesson 16: Blending Short *o* Sound /ŏ/

Say each picture name. Listen to the sounds of the letters as they blend together. Write the picture name on the line.

1 

? o t

hot

2 

? o x

3 

? o p

4 

? o p

5 

? o g

6 

? o x

I Can Do It!

Say each picture name. **Listen** for the short sound of *o*. **Write** the picture name on the line.

1

dog

2

3

4

5

6

7
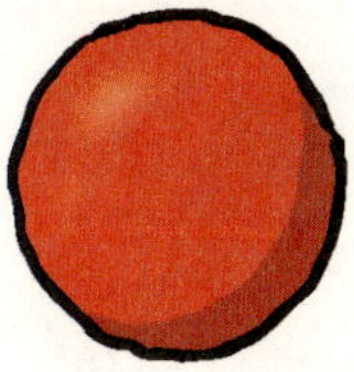

8
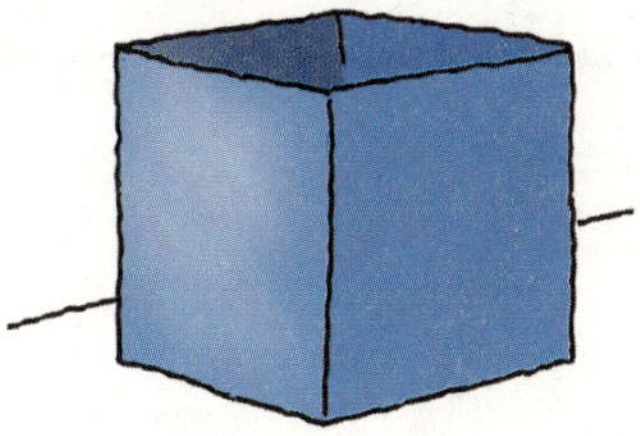

9

Big Idea How do you and your friends help at school?

I Can Do It!

Lesson 17: Writing and Reading Short *o* Sound /ŏ/

Say each picture name. **Listen** for the short sound of *o*. **Fill in** the circle in front of the word that names the picture.

1

● log ○ lip

2

○ bag ○ box

3

○ mom ○ man

4

○ dog ○ dig

5

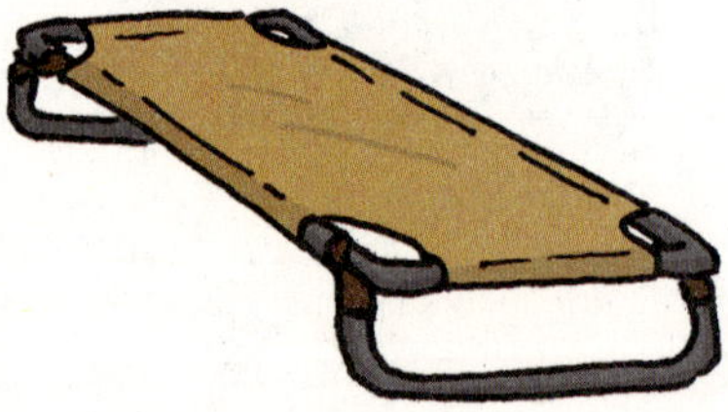

○ cat ○ cot

6

○ pot ○ pit

7

○ fox ○ fix

8

○ mop ○ map

9

○ hip ○ hop

Say each picture name. **Listen** for names that rhyme. **Draw** a line to match the rhyming pictures.

Tongue Twister Brock socks clocks with locks.

Lesson 18: Rhyming Words with Short o Sound /ŏ/

Say each picture name. **Circle** the rhyming pictures. **Write** the rhyming words on the lines.

1

 cot  pot

 cat  cob

cot
pot

2

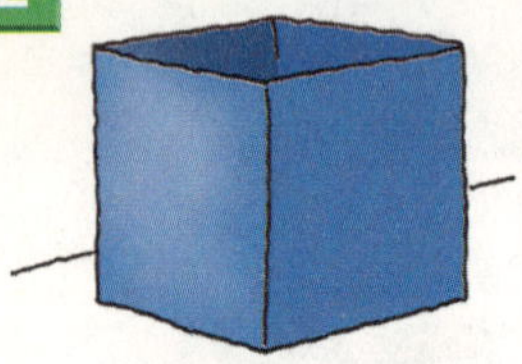 box  six

 fox  top

______
______

3

 mop  Mom

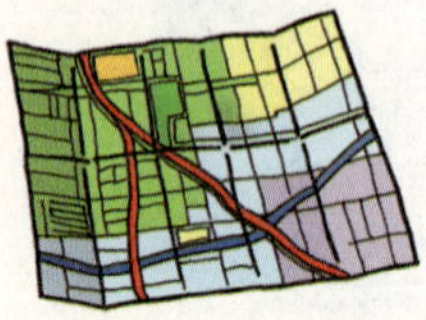 map  hop

______
______

Joke Corner What is a warm circle?

A h_t d_t!

I Can Do It!

Read each sentence. **Fill in** the circle next to the word that makes sense in the sentence. **Write** the word on the line.

1. Don got a big box.
   - ○ hot
   - ● box
   - ○ sod

2. A ______ ran past  .
   - ○ pot
   - ○ hop
   - ○ fox

3. A  can ______ .
   - ○ hop
   - ○ top
   - ○ mop

4. The  is ______ .
   - ○ hot
   - ○ got
   - ○ dot

5. Bob will ______ the  .
   - ○ dot
   - ○ rob
   - ○ pop

6. The  has 3 ______ .
   - ○ pots
   - ○ dots
   - ○ cots

Lesson 19: Using Short o Sound /ŏ/ in Context

Read each sentence. **Write** the sentence that tells about the picture.

1

We sit on top.
We can hop.

We sit on top.

2

The box is on a log.
The box is on a cot.

3

The pig has a cob.
The pig has a cab.

4

Bob has the mop.
Bob has the map.

Review

Read each set of words below. **Combine** words from each set to write three complete sentences.

1

2

3

Think and Link

What help does this clock need?

Tock, tick,
The clock is sick!
Tocks, ticks,
It's always six!

Review

Lesson 20: Review Short *a, i, o* Sounds /ă/, /ĭ/, /ŏ/

Look at each picture. **Read** the words in the box. **Write** sentences about the picture. Use the words in the box to help you.

Bob	dog	Kim	Mom	stop	toss

1

2

I Can Do It!

All-STAR Readers Know

The letter *e* is a vowel. It can stand for the short sound you hear at the beginning of the word *elephant.*

Say each picture name. **Listen** for the short sound of *e*. **Draw** a line from the elephant to each picture that has the short sound of *e*.

Big Idea One way to recycle is to reuse things. What can you reuse at school that will help the environment?

I Can Do It!

Lesson 21: Introducing Short *e* Sound /ĕ/

Say each picture name. **Listen** for the short sound of *e*. **Circle** each picture that has the short sound of *e*.

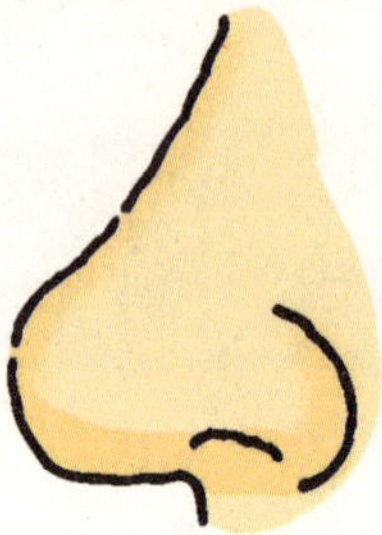

Lesson 22: Identifying Short *e* Sound /ĕ/

I Can Do It!

Say each picture name. **Listen** for the short sound of *e*.
Write *e* under each picture that has the short sound of *e*.

1

e

2

3

4

5

6

7

8

9

Big Idea What are *odd jobs?*

I Can Do It!

Lesson 22: Identifying Short e Sound /ĕ/

Say each picture name. **Listen** for the short sound of *e*. **Write** *e* on the line to complete the word if the picture name has the short sound of *e*.

1

bed

2

h_t

3

10

t_n

4

h_n

5

h_t

6

m_n

7

l_g

8

w_g

9

n_t

I Can Do It!

Say each letter sound. **Blend** the sounds to read the word. **Draw** a line to match the picture to the word that names the picture.

1

ten hen

2

net pet

3

leg beg

4

red bed

5

men pen

6

jet wet

Big Idea How can people help those who need food?

I Can Do It!

Lesson 23: Blending Short *e* Sound /ĕ/

Say each picture name. **Listen** to the sounds of the letters as they blend together. **Write** the picture name on the line.

1 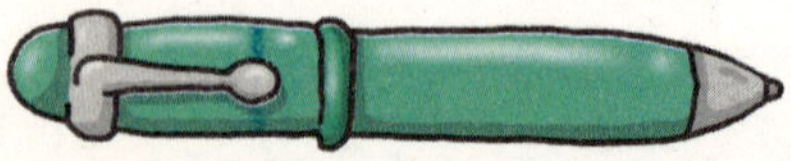

? e n

pen

2 

? e d

3 

? e t

4 

? e t

5 

? e n

6 

? e n

I Can Do It!

Say each picture name. **Listen** for the short sound of *e*. **Write** the picture name on the line.

1

jet

2

3

4

5

6

7

8

9

Think and Link A vet is a helper. How can you help a pet?

I Can Do It!

Lesson 24: Writing and Reading Short *e* Sound /ĕ/

Say each picture name. Listen for the short sound of *e*. Fill in the circle in front of the word that names the picture.

1

● ten ○ net

2

○ jab ○ jet

3

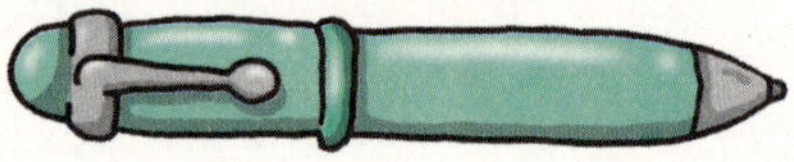

○ pen ○ pan

4

○ wet ○ web

5

○ net ○ nap

6

○ bed ○ bag

7

○ van ○ vet

8

○ leg ○ beg

9

○ set ○ wet

I Can Do It!

Say each picture name. **Listen** for the names that rhyme. **Draw** a line to match the rhyming pictures.

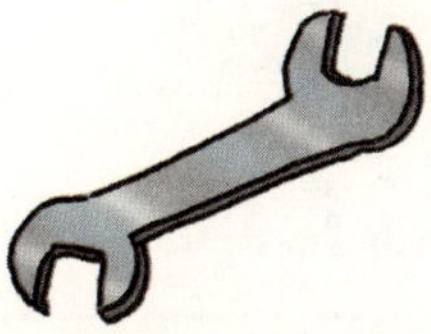

Think and Link Tell a story about a time when you helped someone.

Lesson 25: Rhyming Words with Short e Sound /ĕ/

Say each picture name. Circle the rhyming pictures. Write the rhyming words on the lines.

1

 ten  tan — ten

 red  men — men

2

 net  pet

 pot  pen

3

 bag  leg

 beg  jet

Joke Corner What do you call a soggy animal doctor?

A w_t v_t!

I Can Do It!

Read each sentence. **Fill in** the circle next to the word that makes sense in the sentence. **Write** the word on the line.

1 The bed is .

- ○ big
- ○ bad
- ● bed

2 The  is ____.

- ○ red
- ○ ten
- ○ pen

3 Ben had ____ .

- ○ net
- ○ ten
- ○ men

4 The  has a ____ cat.

- ○ pet
- ○ set
- ○ net

5 The  got ____.

- ○ wet
- ○ red
- ○ bed

6 Ned ____ the .

- ○ red
- ○ bed
- ○ fed

I Can Do It!

Read each sentence. **Write** the sentence that tells about the picture.

1

Ted slips on a log.
Ted slid on a sled.

Ted slid on a sled.

2

Bev sits in the jet.
Bev fits in the bed.

3

The hen has ten eggs.
The dog has tan legs.

4

Ben has a pet bed.
Ben is a wet pet.

Review

Read each set of words below. **Combine** words from each set to write three complete sentences.

1

2

3

Think and Link What kinds of tools would you need to help in a garden?

Review

Look at each picture. **Read** the words in the box. **Write** a sentence about each picture. Use the words in the box to help you.

nest birds sled top hill fed Meg

1

2

I Can Do It!

All-STAR Readers Know

The letter *u* is a vowel. It can stand for the short sound you hear at the beginning of the word *umbrella*. 

Say each picture name. **Listen** for the short sound of *u*. **Color** each picture that has the short sound of *u*.

Rhyme Time

Say the rhyme and listen for words with the short sound of *u*.

Rub-a-dub-dub
Three men in a tub,
And who do you think they be?
The butcher, the baker, the candlestick maker,
All off to sail the sea!

I Can Do It!

Lesson 28: Introducing Short *u* Sound /ŭ/

Look for things that have the short sound of *u*. **Circle** the five things whose names have the short sound of *u*.

Tongue Twister Bugs Buzzard's buzzer bugs Buzz.

I Can Do It!

Say each picture name. Listen for the short sound of *u*.
Write *u* under each picture that has the short sound of *u*.

1

u

2

3

4

5

6

7

8

9

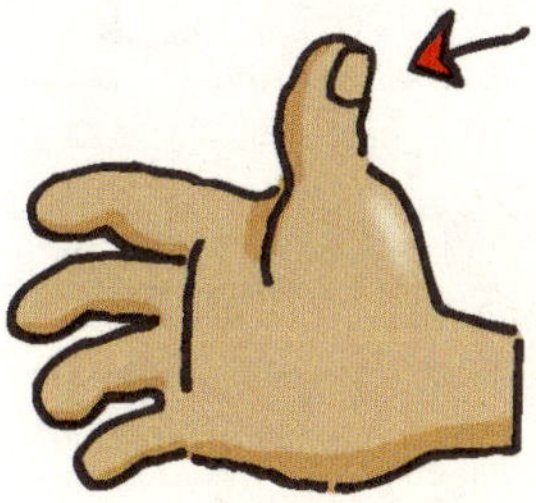

On-Track Fact Have you heard of the Red Cross? What other groups do you know that help people?

I Can Do It!

Lesson 29: Identifying Short *u* Sound /ŭ/

Say each picture name. **Listen** for the short sound of *u* in the middle of the word. **Write** *u* on the line to complete the word if the picture name has the short sound of *u*.

1 

b u g

2 

c __ p

3 

f __ n

4 

r __ g

5 

t __ n

6 

b __ n

7 

c __ t

8 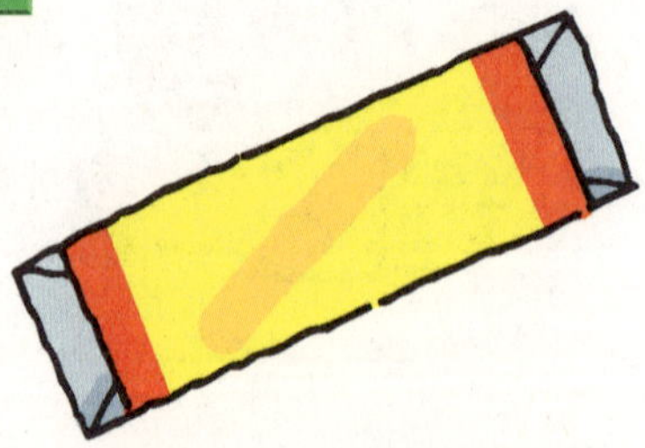

g __ m

9 

n __ t

I Can Do It!

Say each letter sound. **Blend** the sounds to read the word. **Draw** a line to match the picture to the word that names the picture.

1

bug hug

4

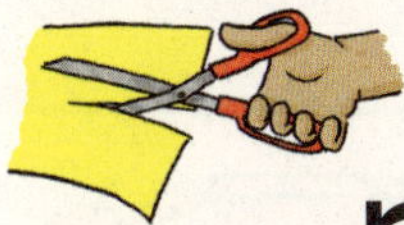

cut nut

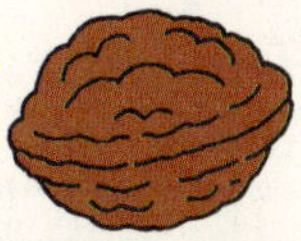

2

cup pup

5

sun bun

3

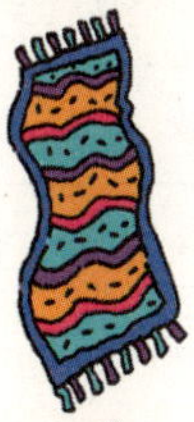

mug rug

6

cub sub

Big Idea How can children be helpers?

I Can Do It!

Lesson 30: Blending Short *u* Sound /ŭ/

Say each picture name. **Listen** to the sounds of the letters as they blend together. **Write** the picture name on the line.

1 

? u g

rug

2 

? u p

3 

? u n

4 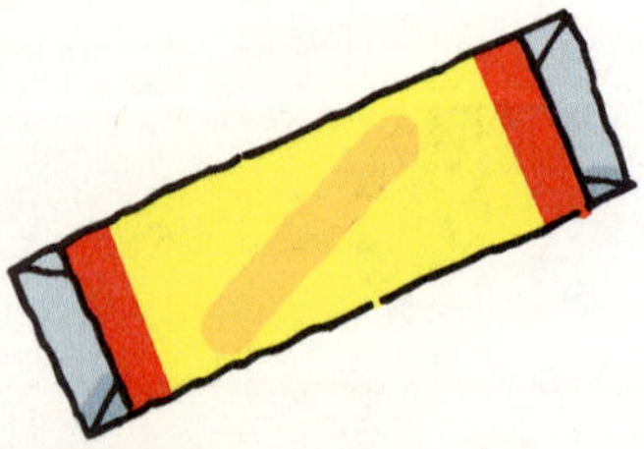

? u m

5 

? u b

6 

? u n

I Can Do It!

Say each picture name. **Listen** for the short sound of *u*. **Write** the picture name on the line.

1
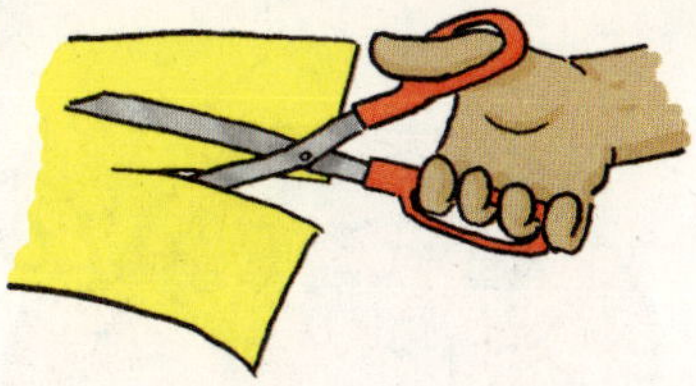
cut

2

3

4

5

6

7

8

9

Joke Corner What do you call a cup for a grasshopper?

A b__g m__g!

I Can Do It!

Lesson 31: Writing and Reading Short *u* Sound /ŭ/

Say each picture name. **Listen** for the short sound of *u*. **Fill in** the circle in front of the word that names the picture.

1

● nut ○ net

2

○ bun ○ bin

3

○ hug ○ bug

4

○ cub ○ tub

5

○ sun ○ sub

6

○ rub ○ run

7

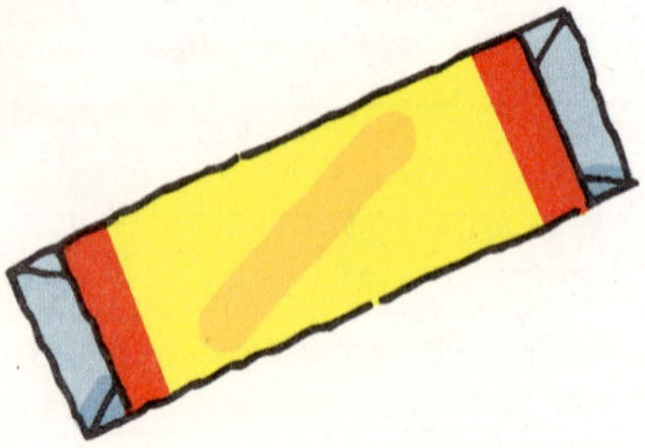

○ gum ○ hum

8

○ pup ○ cup

9

○ mud ○ mug

I Can Do It!

Say each picture name. Listen for names that rhyme.
Draw a line to match the rhyming pictures.

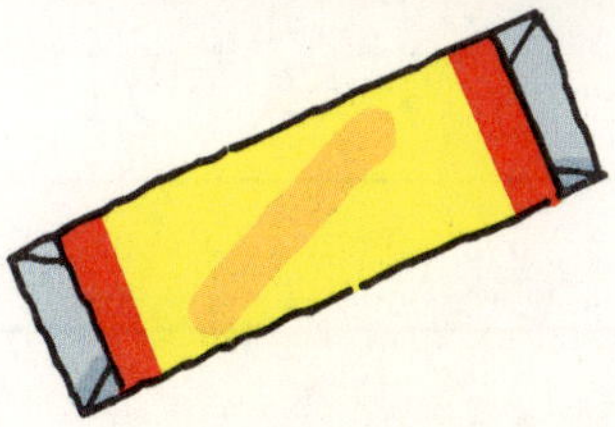

I Can Do It!

Lesson 32: Rhyming Words with Short *u* Sound /ŭ/

Say each picture name. **Circle** the rhyming pictures. **Write** the rhyming words on the lines.

1

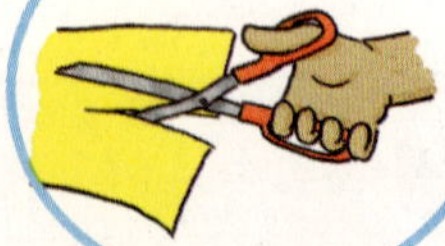 cut  nut

 net  bun

cut

nut

2

 man  run

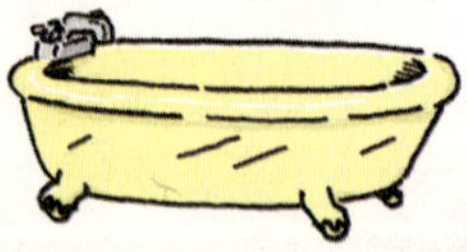 tub  sun

3

 rug  bus

 bag  bug

Joke Corner What boat do you take a bath in?

A t__b s__b!

I Can Do It!

Read each sentence. **Fill in** the circle next to the word that makes sense in the sentence. **Write** the word on the line.

1 The  sits on a bus.

- ○ bun
- ● bus
- ○ bud

2 A  sat in a ____.

- ○ bud
- ○ bun
- ○ tub

3 Andy had ____ .

- ○ run
- ○ fun
- ○ bun

4 A  ran up a ____.

- ○ nut
- ○ fun
- ○ cup

5  can ____ the pup.

- ○ hug
- ○ hum
- ○ fun

6 A  needs the ____.

- ○ rub
- ○ sun
- ○ bun

I Can Do It!

Lesson 33: Using Short *u* Sound /ŭ/ in Context

Read each sentence. **Write** the sentence that tells about the picture.

1

The bug can bun.
The bug can buzz.

The bug can buzz.

2

The mug is hot.
The mud is hot.

3

A pup dug in the mud.
The mud is on the bud.

4

The sun is red.
The sun is up.

Review

Say each picture name. **Listen** for the short vowel sound. **Write** the vowel on the line to complete the word.

1

log

2

t__n

3

h__t

4
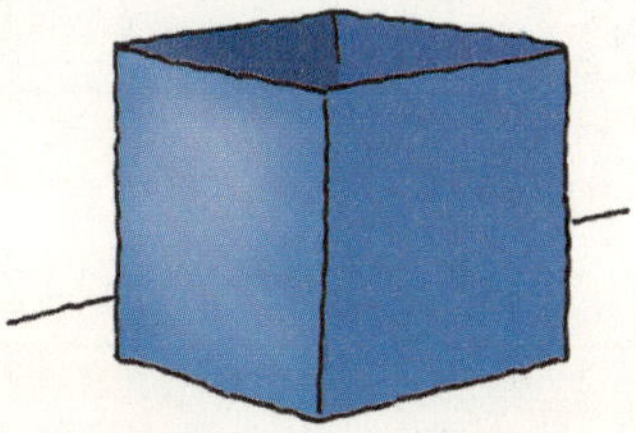
b__x

5

n__t

6

c__p

7

f__n

8
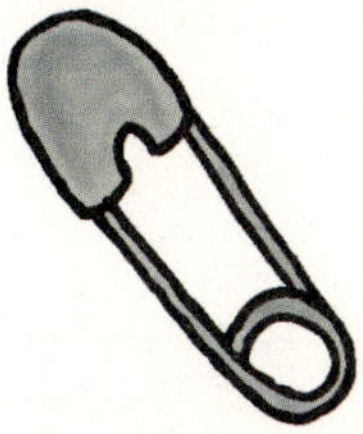
p__n

9

b__g

Review

Lesson 34: Review Short Vowel Sounds

Say each picture name. **Listen** for the short vowel sound. **Write** the picture name on the line.

1 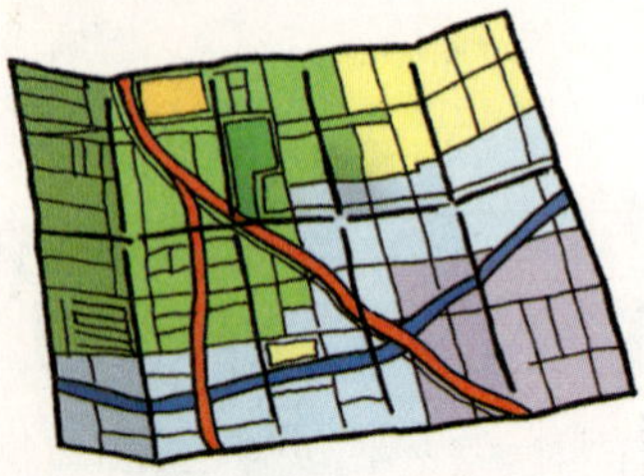

map

2 

3 

4 

5 

6 

7 

8 

9 

Think and Link Which would you most like to help someone do? Why?

○ **mop**

○ **shop**

Read each set of words below. Combine words from each set to write three complete sentences.

1

2

3

Rhyme Time

Splish, splash,
Splish, splash,
Drip, drop,
Drip, drop,
Will the rain ever stop?

Lesson 34: Review Short Vowel Sounds

Review

Look at each picture. **Read** the words in the box. **Write** a sentence about each picture. Use the words in the box to help you.

fun	have	dog	jump	spots	can

1

2

I Can Read It!

Read the poem. Listen for words with short vowel sounds.

from *The Lorax*

by Dr. Seuss

Unless someone like you
cares a whole awful lot,
nothing is going to get better.
It's not.

Circle the three words that have the short *e* sound /ĕ/.

Write about one thing that could be better in the world.

I Can Write It!

Lesson 36: Writing

Think about how you might help someone at home. **Draw** what you might do. **Write** about your picture on the lines. The words in the box can help you.

help	can	pick	up	sit	get

At Home Read your child's description together. Have your child identify words with short vowel sounds.

Grandpa's Helper

This book belongs to

Then I can put food into
the dog's dish.

Grandpa Sam is happy when
I water the plants.

I will be back soon to help again!

I can give Grandpa Sam's dog a bath.

2

It is fun to help Grandpa Sam.

7

Next I help Grandpa Sam wash his windows.

4

Then we fix lunch. Grandpa Sam makes fun zig-zag sandwiches!

5

When I Grow Up

poem for rodney

by Nikki Giovanni

people always ask what
am i going to be
when i grow
up and i always
just think
i'd like to grow
up

On My Mind

What do you want to be like when you grow up?

All-STARs at Home

Dear Family,

Our class is beginning Unit 4 of *SRA All-STAR Phonics.* The theme of this unit is "When I Grow Up." The skill focus is long vowel sounds. Some words with long vowel sounds include *rain, feet, pie, boat, use* and *tune.* Try some of the following fun activities to help your child become familiar with these sounds.

★ **Sound Cards:** Help your child look in magazines or coloring books for pictures whose names have long vowel sounds. Paste these on cards and put them in a pile. Have your child choose two cards at a time. Ask him or her to say the picture names. If both cards have the same vowel sound, your child can keep the cards. If not, the cards are returned to the pile. Over time, add cards to the set.

★ **When I Grow Up:** Together, make a list of jobs your child thinks may be interesting. As your child says each word, ask him or her to tell you if that word has a long vowel sound. If it does, have your child circle the word on the list.

★ Look for books about growing up in the library or bookstore. We suggest:

- *Oh, Grow Up! Poems to Help You Survive Parents, Chores, School and Other Afflictions* by Florence Parry Heide, Orchard Books, 1996.
- *When I Grow Up* by Fran Newman D'Amico, Dover Publications, 2001.

All-STAR Readers Know

The letter *a* is a vowel.

- It can stand for the short *a* sound /ă/ in *can.* 

- It can stand for the long *a* sound /ā/ in *cane.* 

Say each picture name. **Listen** for the long *a* sound /ā/. **Circle** each picture whose name has the long *a* sound /ā/.

Think and Link What did you look like when you were a baby? How are you different now? How are you the same? (Circle the two long *a* sounds.)

I Can Do It!

Lesson 1: Introducing Long *a* Sound /ā/

Say each picture name. **Listen** to the sound of *a*.
Circle ā if you hear the long *a* sound /ā/, as in *cake*.
Circle ă if you hear the short *a* sound /ă/, as in *cat*.

1 

ā ă

2 

ā ă

3 

ā ă

4 

ā ă

5 

ā ă

6 

ā ă

7 

ā ă

8 

ā ă

9 

ā ă

10 

ā ă

11 

ā ă

12 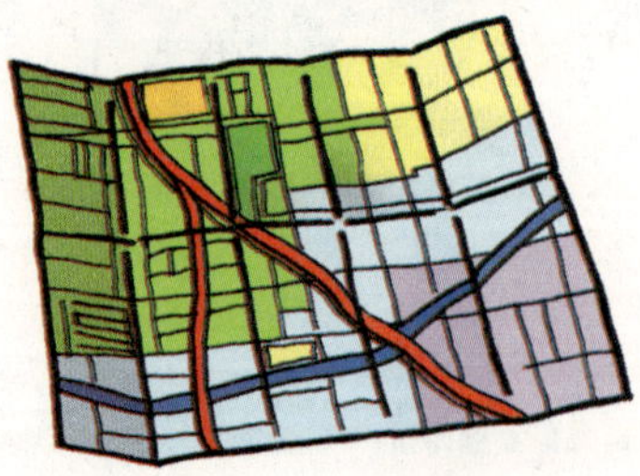

ā ă

I Can Do It!

All-STAR Readers Know

In words like *cane* and *rake*, the *a* stands for the long *a* sound /ā/ and the *e* is silent.

Say each picture name. **Listen** for the long *a* sound /ā/. **Write** *e* at the end of the word if you hear the long *a* sound /ā/.

1 

cane

2 

tap__

3 

pan__

4 

man__

5 

bat__

6 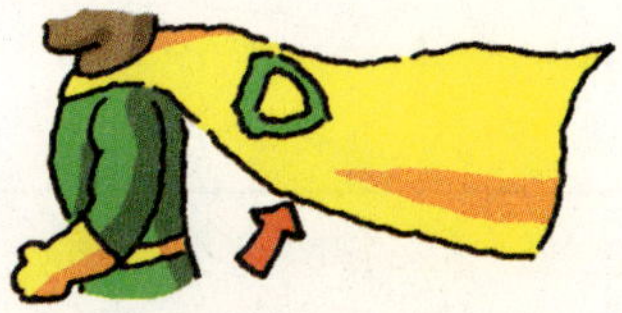

cap__

7 

van__

8 

pan__

9 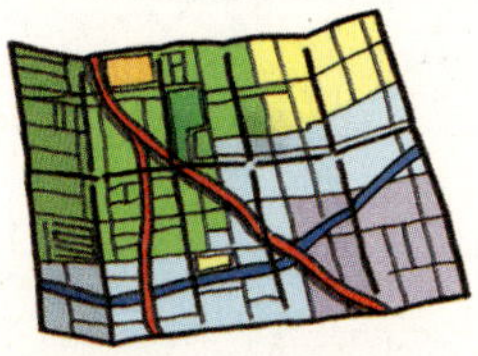

map__

I Can Do It!

Lesson 2: Identifying Long *a* Sound /ā/

Say each picture name. Circle the word that names the picture. Write the picture name on the line. Hint: Some picture names have the short *a* sound /ă/, and some picture names have the long *a* sound /ā/.

1 

can cane

cane

2 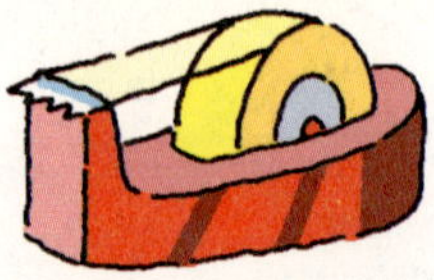

tap tape

3 

van vane

4 

pan pane

5 

man mane

6 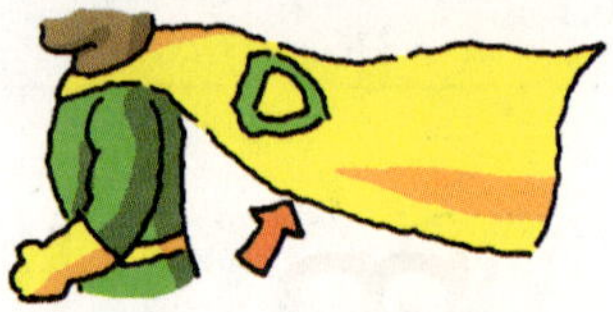

cap cape

7 

pan pane

8 

can cane

9 

man mane

Big Idea What are some things you can do now that you could not do when you were younger?

I Can Do It!

All-STAR Readers Know

The letters *ai* usually stand for the long *a* sound /ā/, as in *rain* and *sail.*

Say each picture name. **Listen** for the long *a* sound /ā/. **Write** *ai* on the line if you hear the long *a* sound /ā/.

1 

mail

2 

m___n

3 

p___d

4 

m___d

5 

t___l

6 

r___n

7 

p___l

8 

n___l

9 

p___n

I Can Do It!

All-STAR Readers Know

The letters *ay* usually stand for the long *a* sound /ā/, as in *day* and *say*.

Say each picture name. **Circle** the word that names the picture. **Write** the picture name on the line. Hint: Some picture names have the short *a* sound /ă/, and some picture names have the long *a* sound /ā/.

1 

(jay) jam

jay

2 

hay hat

3 

bay bag

4 

man may

5 

say sat

6 

mad sad

7 

day dad

8 

pay pan

9 

ray ram

I Can Do It!

Say each picture name. Draw a line to match the pictures whose names rhyme.

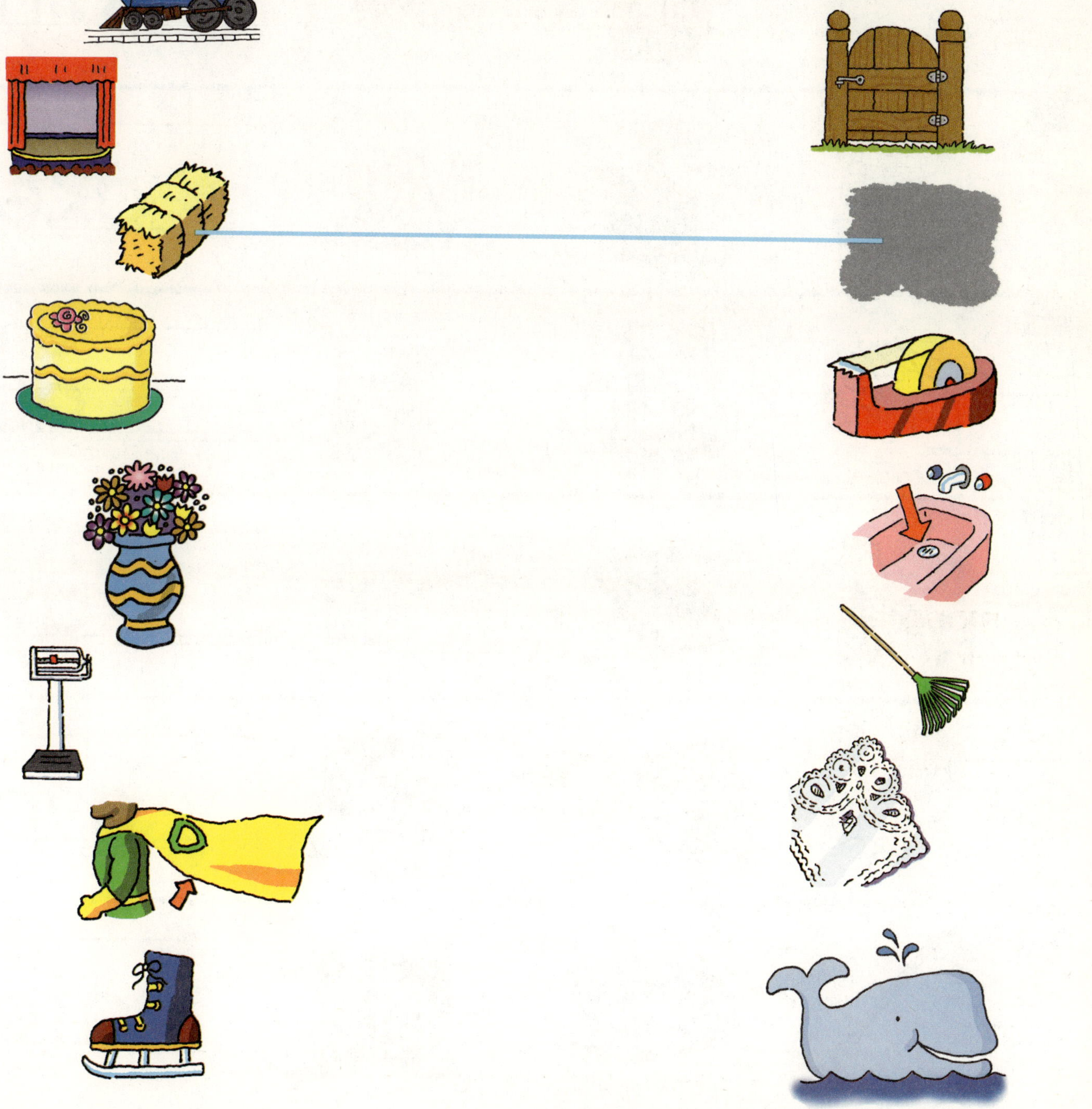

Tongue Twister Ray raced in the rain.

I Can Do It!

Lesson 4: Rhyming Words with Long *a* Sound /ā/

Say each picture name. **Circle** the pictures whose names rhyme. **Write** one more rhyming word by filling in the blank letter.

1

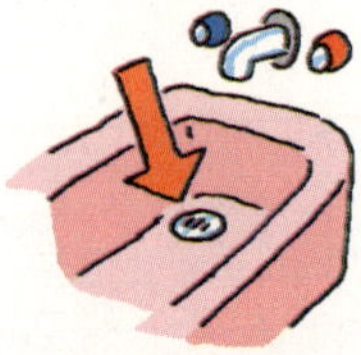
___ain

2

___ake

3

___ail

4

___ay

5

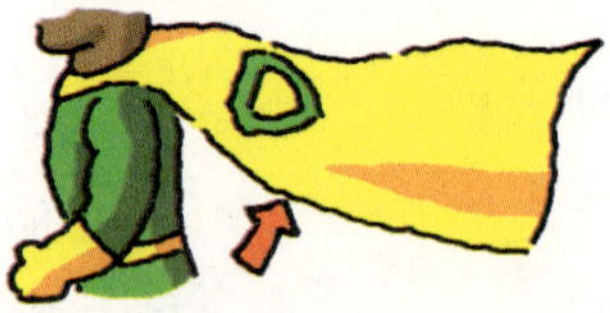

___ave

6

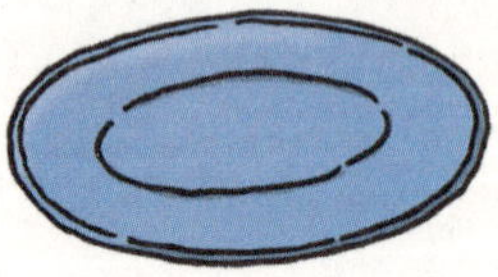

___ate

Big Idea What is the best grown-up age? Why?

Read each sentence. **Fill in** the circle next to the word that best completes the sentence. **Write** the word on the line.

1. Ray is late for .
   - ○ lane
   - ● late
   - ○ lake

2. Kate  on the ______.
   - ○ bay
   - ○ bake
   - ○ bat

3. Dad will ______ a .
   - ○ bake
   - ○ base
   - ○ bat

4. Don't ______ the .
   - ○ wade
   - ○ wait
   - ○ wake

5. The ______ fell 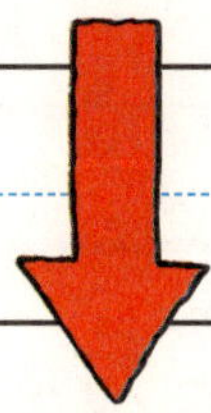.
   - ○ raid
   - ○ rain
   - ○ rail

6. I will ______ a .
   - ○ mane
   - ○ make
   - ○ map

I Can Do It!

Lesson 5: Using Long *a* Sound /ā/ in Context

Read each sentence. Write the sentence that tells about the picture.

1

Mom can bake a cake.
Mom can play a game.

Mom can bake a cake.

2

Dave put a rake by the lake.
The rake is by a gate.

3

I put tape on a pane.
The pane has a cape.

4

Deb will play in the rain.
Deb will sail on a lake.

I Can Do It!

All-STAR Readers Know

The letter *i* is a vowel.

- It can stand for the short *i* sound /ĭ/ in *pin.* 
- It can stand for the long *i* sound /ī/ in *pine.* 

Say each picture name. **Listen** for the long *i* sound /ī/.
Circle each picture whose name has the long *i* sound /ī/.

Rhyme Time Circle four words with the long *i* sound /ī/ in this rhyme.

Mike likes to bike and hike.

I Can Do It!

Lesson 6: Introducing Long *i* Sound /ī/

Say each picture name. Listen to the sound of *i*.
Circle ī if you hear the long *i* sound /ī/, as in *pine*.
Circle ĭ if you hear the short *i* sound /ĭ/, as in *pin*.

1

ī ĭ

2

ī ĭ

3

ī ĭ

4

ī ĭ

5

ī ĭ

6

ī ĭ

7

ī ĭ

8

ī ĭ

9
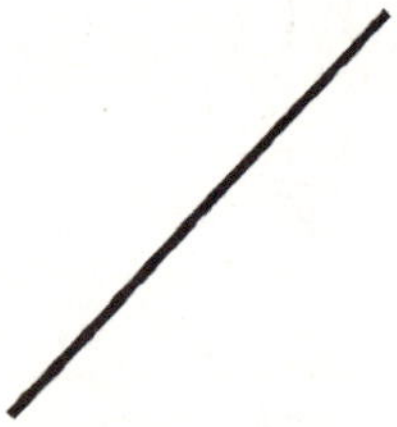
ī ĭ

10

ī ĭ

11

ī ĭ

12

ī ĭ

I Can Do It!

All-STAR Readers Know

In words like *fine* and *mine*, the *i* stands for the long *i* sound /ī/ and the *e* is silent.

Say each picture name. **Listen** for the long *i* sound /ī/. **Write** *e* at the end of the word if you hear the long *i* sound /ī/.

1

dime

2

pin__

3

bik__

4

nin__

5

pin__

6

kit__

7

pig__

8

fin__

9

fiv__

Lesson 7: Identifying Long *i* Sound /ī/

Say each picture name. **Circle** the word that names the picture. **Write** the picture name on the line.
Hint: Some picture names have the short *i* sound /ĭ/, and some picture names have the long *i* sound /ī/.

1. 
   rid (ride)
   ride

2. 
   pin pine

3. 
   lip line

4. 
   pin pine

5. 
   hit hive

6. 
   nine nip

7. 
   sit site

8. 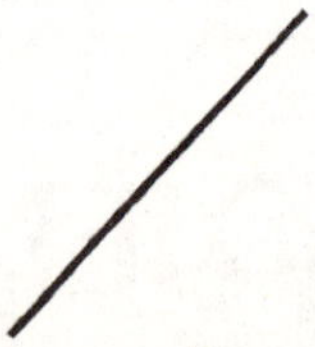
   fin line

9. 
   kite kit

Phonics Focus The letter *y* can stand for the long *i* sound /ī/, as in *my* and *by.*

Lesson 8: Rhyming Words with Long *i* Sound /ī/

I Can Do It!

Say each picture name.
Draw a line to match the pictures whose names rhyme.

Think and Link Think of a grown-up you like. Complete this sentence with a grown-up's name.

I like ____________________.

I Can Do It!

Lesson 8: Rhyming Words with Long *i* Sound /ī/

Say each picture name. **Circle** the pictures whose names rhyme. **Write** one more rhyming word by filling in the blank letter.

1  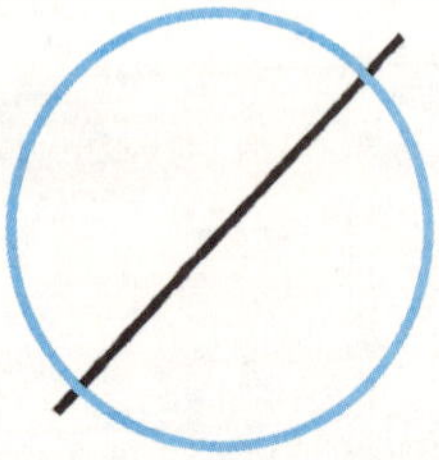  ___ine

2 

  ___ime

3    ___ide

4    ___ive

5    ___ice

Tongue Twister Nice mice like nice ice.

Review

Read each set of words below. **Combine** words from each set to write three complete sentences.

1

2

3

Think and Link What kind of job can you have if you like animals?

Review

Look at each picture. **Read** the words in the box. **Write** sentences about the picture using the words in the box for help.

rain kite fine play time take

1

2

Riddle Time What do you call a green watch?

l_me t_me

I Can Do It!

All-STAR Readers Know

The letter *o* is a vowel.

- It can stand for the short *o* sound /ŏ/ in *box*. 
- It can stand for the long *o* sound /ō/ in *boat*. 

Say each picture name. **Listen** for the long *o* sound /ō/. **Circle** each picture whose name has the long *o* sound /ō/.

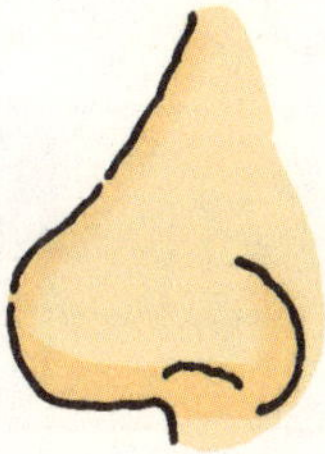

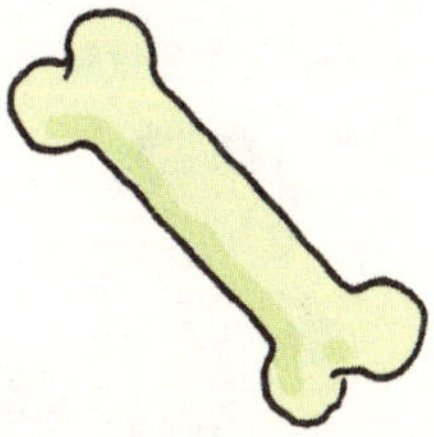

Think and Link What jobs can you think of whose names have a short *o* or long *o* sound?

I Can Do It!

Lesson 10: Introducing Long *o* Sound /ō/

Say each picture name. **Listen** to the sound of *o*.
Circle ō if you hear the long *o* sound /ō/, as in *boat*.
Circle ŏ if you hear the short *o* sound /ŏ/, as in *box*.

1

ō ŏ

2

ō ŏ

3

ō ŏ

4

ō ŏ

5

ō ŏ

6

ō ŏ

7

ō ŏ

8

ō ŏ

9

ō ŏ

10

ō ŏ

11

ō ŏ

12

ō ŏ

I Can Do It!

All-STAR Readers Know

In words like *note* and *joke,* the *o* stands for the long *o* sound /ō/ and the *e* is silent.

Say each picture name. **Listen** for the long *o* sound /ō/.
Write *e* at the end of the word if you hear the long *o* sound /ō/.

1 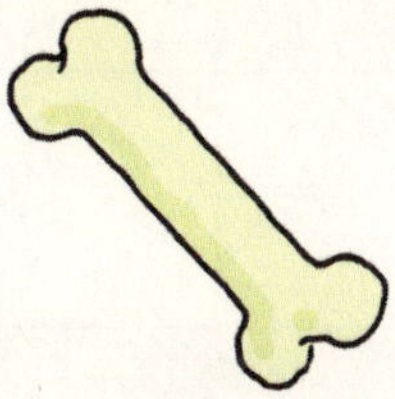

bone

2 

hop___

3 

hos___

4 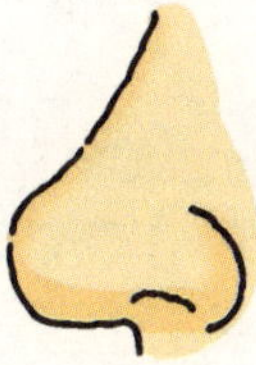

nos___

5 

con___

6 

mop___

7 

pol___

8 

cot___

9 

rop___

I Can Do It!

Lesson 11: Identifying Long *o* Sound /ō/

Say each picture name. **Circle** the word that names the picture. **Write** the picture name on the line.
Hint: Some picture names have the short *o* sound /ŏ/, and some picture names have the long *o* sound /ō/.

1

con (cone)

cone

2

ros rose

3

pok poke

4

hop hope

5

rob robe

6

mop mope

7

nos nose

8

not note

9

top tone

I Can Do It!

All-STAR Readers Know

The letters *oa* usually stand for the long *o* sound /ō/, as in *load* and *goal*.

Say each picture name. **Listen** for the long *o* sound /ō/. **Write** *oa* on the line if you hear the long *o* sound /ō/.

1 

g oa t

2 

h ___ p

3 

s ___ p

4 

c ___ t

5 

d ___ g

6 

t ___ d

7 

f ___ x

8 

r ___ d

9 

b ___ t

I Can Do It!

All-STAR Readers Know

The letters *ow* sometimes stand for the long *o* sound /ō/, as in *grow* and *blow*.

Say each picture name. **Circle** the word that names the picture. **Write** the picture name on the line. Hint: Some picture names have the short *o* sound /ŏ/, and some picture names have the long *o* sound /ō/.

1 

sob snow

snow

2 

got grow

3 

box boat

4 

mad mow

5 

hot hat

6 

bag blow

7 

box bow

8 

pot tow

9 

cot crow

I Can Do It!

Say each picture name. Draw a line to match the pictures whose names rhyme.

Big Idea What do you like about school this year? What do you think next year will be like?

I Can Do It!

Say each picture name. **Circle** the pictures whose names rhyme. **Write** one more rhyming word by filling in the blank letter.

1

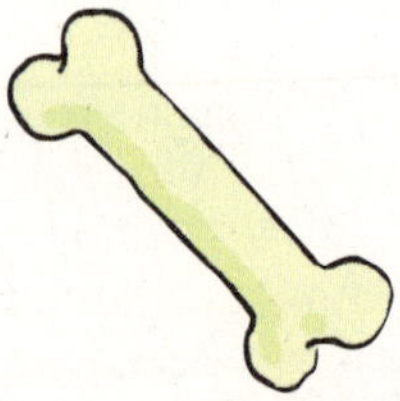
___oat

2

___ow

3

___oke

4

___oad

5

___ose

Tongue Twister Sally soaks boats, goats, and coats.

Review

Read each set of words below. **Combine** the words from each set to write three complete sentences.

1

The goat
Jane
Mike

2

will sail
can hide
rode

3

Think and Link If a firefighter came to your class, what questions would you ask?

Review

Lesson 14: Review Long *a, i, o* Sounds /ā/, /ī/, /ō/

Look at each picture. **Read** the words in the box. **Write** sentences about the picture using the words in the box for help.

bike	like	race	road
bone	play	ride	throw

1

2

I Can Do It!

All-STAR Readers Know

The letter *e* is a vowel.

- It can stand for the short *e* sound /ĕ/ in *bed.* 
- It can stand for the long *e* sound /ē/ in *bead.* 

Say each picture name. **Listen** for the long *e* sound /ē/.
Circle each picture whose name has the long *e* sound /ē/.

Phonics Focus The letter *y* can stand for the long *e* sound /ē/, as in *baby* and *penny.*

I Can Do It!

Lesson 15: Introducing Long e Sound /ē/

Say each picture name. Listen to the sound of *e*.
Circle ē if you hear the long *e* sound /ē/, as in *bead*.
Circle ĕ if you hear the short *e* sound /ĕ/, as in *bed*.

1

ē ĕ

2

ē ĕ

3

ē ĕ

4

ē ĕ

5

ē ĕ

6

ē ĕ

7

ē ĕ

8

ē ĕ

9

ē ĕ

10
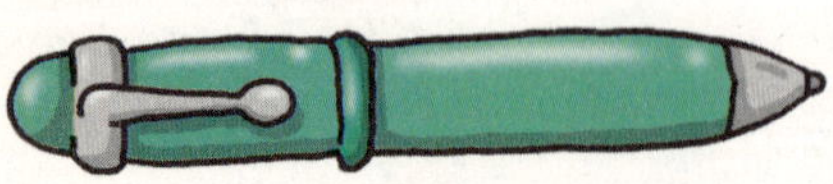
ē ĕ

11

ē ĕ

12

ē ĕ

I Can Do It!

All-STAR Readers Know

The letters *ea* usually stand for the long *e* sound /ē/, as in *meat* and *seat*.

Say each picture name. **Circle** the word that names the picture. **Write** the picture name on the line. Hint: Some picture names have the short *e* sound /ĕ/, and some picture names have the long *e* sound /ē/.

1

pet (peas)

peas

2

loaf leaf

3

Ben bean

4

side seal

5

jet jeans

6

men meal

Tongue Twister Beans and peas please.

I Can Do It!

All-STAR Readers Know

The letters *ee* usually stand for the long *e* sound /ē/, as in *keep* and *see.*

Say each picture name. **Listen** for the long *e* sound /ē/. **Write** *ee* on the line if you hear the long *e* sound /ē/.

1 

tr**ee**

2 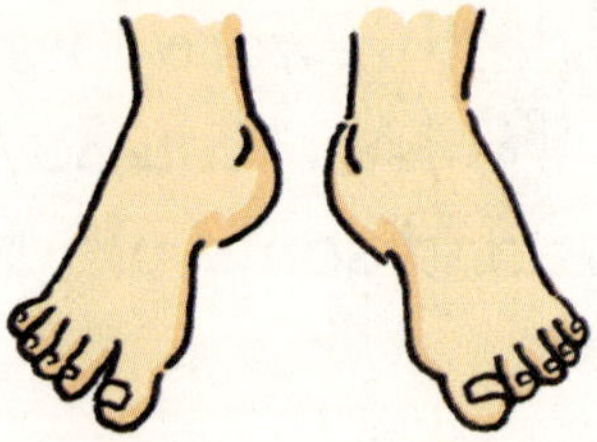

f__t

3 

t__n

4 

gr__n

5 

b__d

6 

wh__l

7 

sl__d

8 

b__

9 

s__d

I Can Do It!

Say each picture name. **Draw** a line to match the pictures whose names rhyme.

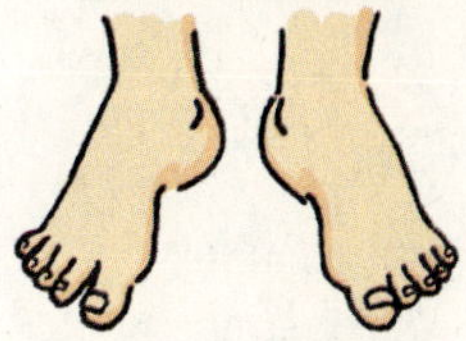

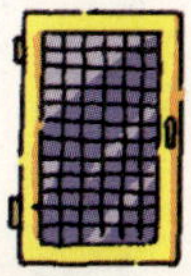

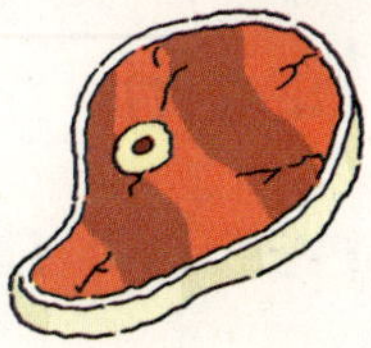

Rhyme Time Say this rhyme. Circle the six words with the long *e* sound /ē/.

Jake and Lee
Went up a tree.
Up, up, up
So they could see.
What did they see?
A tree! A tree!

I Can Do It!

Lesson 17: Rhyming Words with Long *e* Sound /ē/

Say each picture name. **Read** the words. **Circle** the words that rhyme with the picture's name.

1

bee	bed
pie	key
see	red

2

feel	meal
keep	peel
fed	seal

3

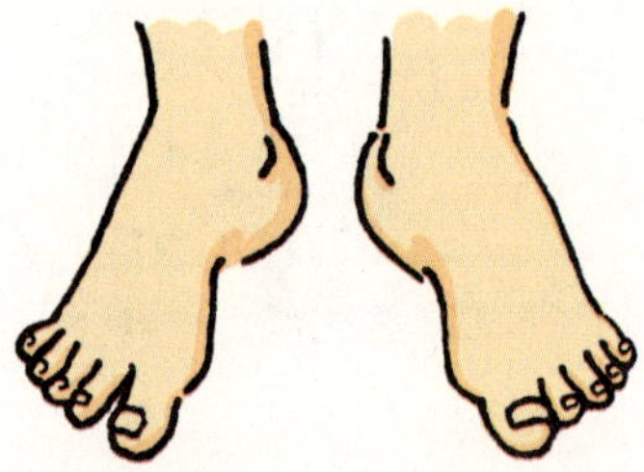

bean	beet
beam	meet
neat	bet

4

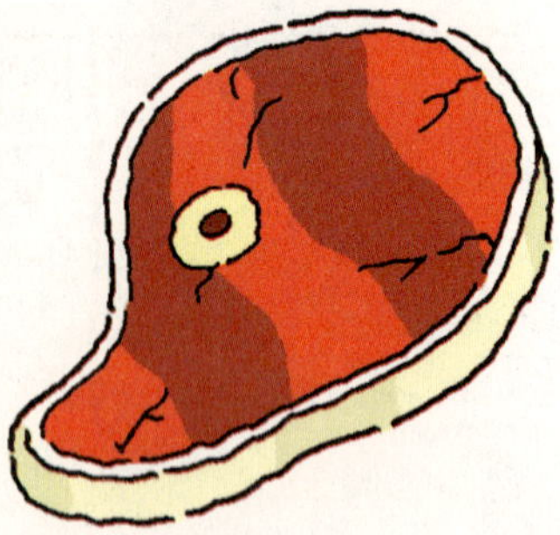

eat	feet
heat	wet
pet	seat

5

hen	Jean
mean	bean
lean	pen

6

keep	beep
home	leap
peep	ripe

Review

Say each picture name. **Fill** in the circle in front of the word that names the picture. **Write** the word on the line.

1

○ goat
● coat
○ cot

coat

2

○ rain
○ ran
○ mane

3

○ kite
○ bake
○ bike

4

○ cake
○ lake
○ cane

5

○ real
○ red
○ read

6

○ boat
○ bat
○ bone

7

○ heel
○ leaf
○ lean

8

○ five
○ hide
○ hive

9

○ tap
○ tape
○ take

Review

Lesson 18: Review Long *a, i, o, e* Sounds /ā/, /ī/, /ō/, /ē/

Read each sentence. **Fill** in the circle next to the word that best completes the sentence. **Write** the word on the line.

1. The hose is five  .
   - ● hose
   - ○ hope
   - ○ hole

2. It's ________ to eat  .
   - ○ tide
   - ○ time
   - ○ tire

3. Please ________ my  .
   - ○ fed
   - ○ feed
   - ○ feet

4. Joan will ________  .
   - ○ hay
   - ○ pay
   - ○ play

5. We ________ in the  .
   - ○ hive
   - ○ pile
   - ○ hike

6. My ________ has no  .
   - ○ coat
   - ○ goat
   - ○ cat

Review

Read each set of words below. **Combine** words from each set to write three complete sentences.

1	2	3
The bee	has a home	in a tree.
Kate	likes to read	at the bay.
Dean	can soak	on a boat.

Riddle Time What do you call a bad seed?

A m__n b__n!

Review

Lesson 18: Review Long *a, i, o, e* Sounds /ā/, /ī/, /ō/, /ē/

Look at each picture. **Read** the words in the box. **Write** sentences about the picture using the words in the box for help.

read	sea	seat	ride
seal	day	five	road

1

2

I Can Do It!

All-STAR Readers Know

The letter *u* is a vowel.

- It can stand for the short *u* sound /ŭ/ in *cub.* 
- It can stand for the two long *u* sounds /ū/ in *cube* 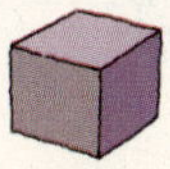 or *glue.* 

Say each picture name. **Listen** for the long *u* sound /ū/.
Circle each picture whose name has the long *u* sound /ū/.

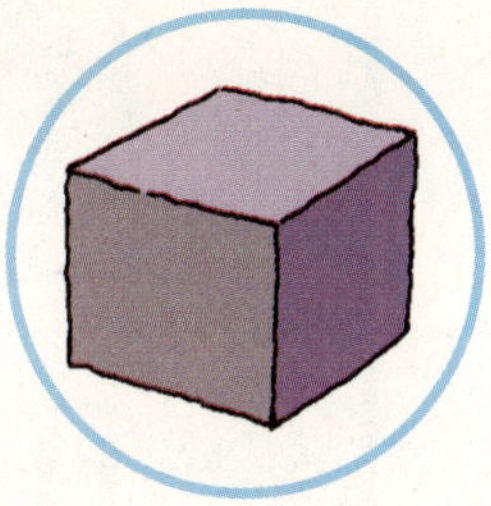

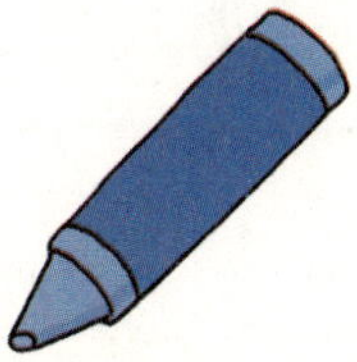

Big Idea What are some jobs you could have if you like to make things?

I Can Do It!

Lesson 19: Introducing Long *u* Sound /ū/

Say each picture name. **Listen** to the sound of *u*. **Circle** ū if you hear the long *u* sound /ū/, as in *cube* or *glue*. **Circle** ŭ if you hear the short *u* sound /ŭ/, as in *cub*.

1 

ū ŭ

2 

ū ŭ

3 

ū ŭ

4 

ū ŭ

5 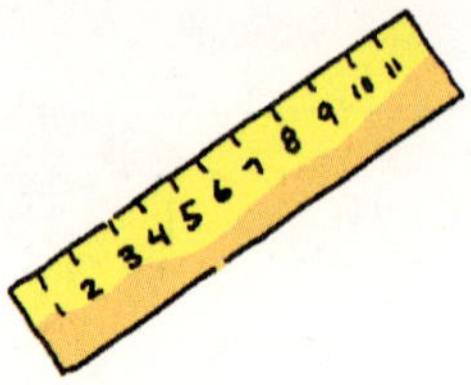

ū ŭ

6 

ū ŭ

7 

ū ŭ

8 

ū ŭ

9 

ū ŭ

10 

ū ŭ

11 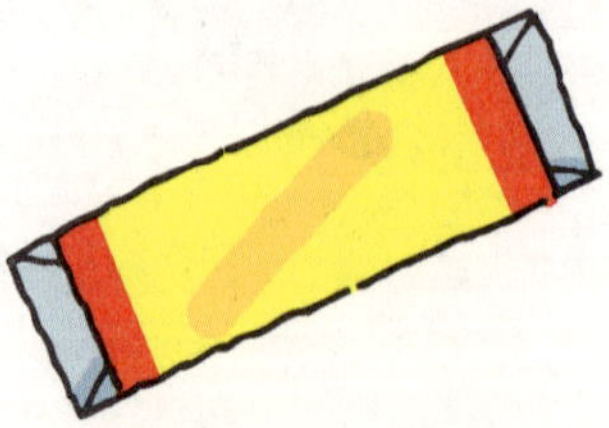

ū ŭ

12 

ū ŭ

I Can Do It!

All-STAR Readers Know

In words like *tube* and *cute*, the *u* stands for the long *u* sound /ū/ and the *e* is silent.

Say each picture name. **Listen** for the long sound of *u*. **Write** *e* at the end of the word if you hear the long *u* sound /ū/.

1 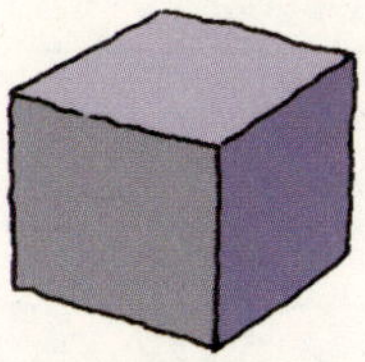

cube

2 

tub___

3 

mul___

4 

bug___

5 

rug___

6 

glu___

7 

tub___

8 

bus___

9 

blu___

I Can Do It!

Lesson 20: Identifying Long *u* Sound /ū/

Say each picture name. **Circle** the word that names the picture. **Write** the picture name on the line.
Hint: Some picture names have the short *u* sound /ŭ/, and some picture names have the long *u* sound /ū/.

1

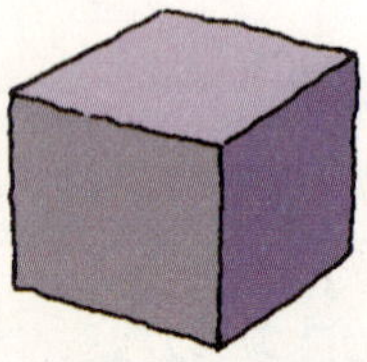

cub cube

cube

2

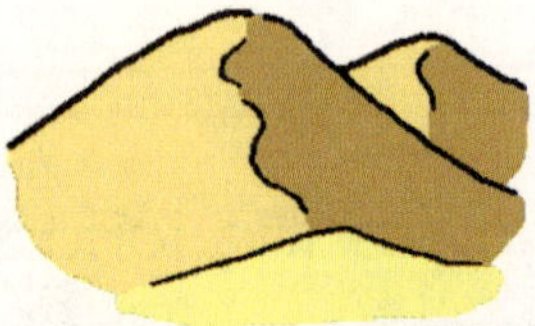

den dune

3

tub tube

4

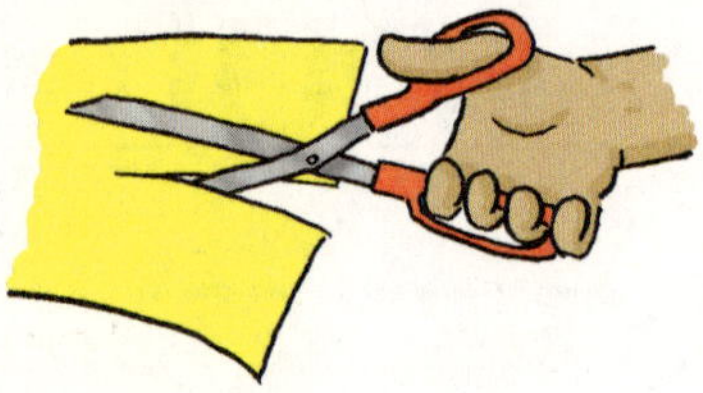

cut cute

5

bulb blue

6

tub tube

7

mull mule

8

hug huge

9

us use

Lesson 21: Review Long Vowel Sounds

Review

Say each picture name. **Fill** in the circle in front of each picture name. **Write** the picture name on the line.

1

- road
- rod
- rope

road

2

- mole
- mule
- mile

3

- rake
- rain
- rail

4

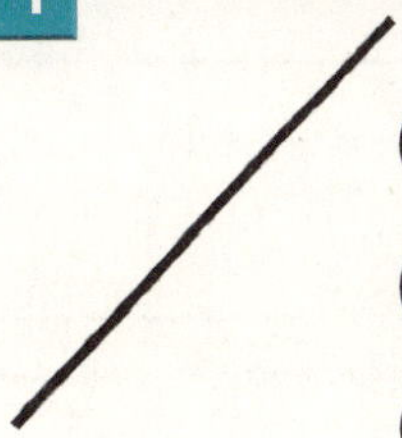

- vine
- fine
- line

5

- feed
- seed
- seal

6

- note
- neat
- tone

7

- bee
- wide
- week

8

- dune
- dime
- mine

9

- goat
- late
- gate

Big Idea What is something you can teach a younger child to do?

Review

Lesson 21: Review Long Vowel Sounds

Say each picture name.
Write the picture name on the line.

feet	cube	tube	bone
rain	five	kite	hay
soap	meat	bowl	game

1 

2 

3 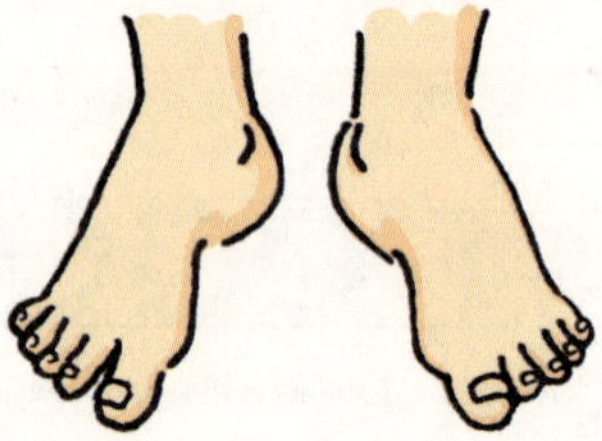

4 

5 

6 

7 

8 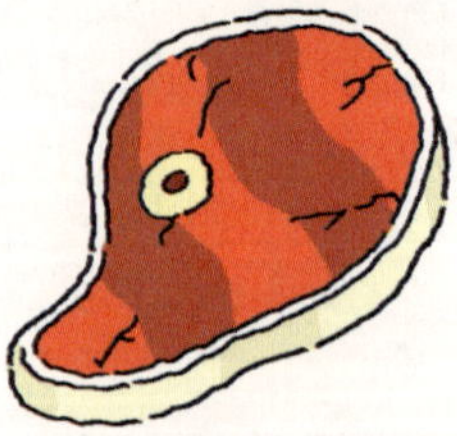

9 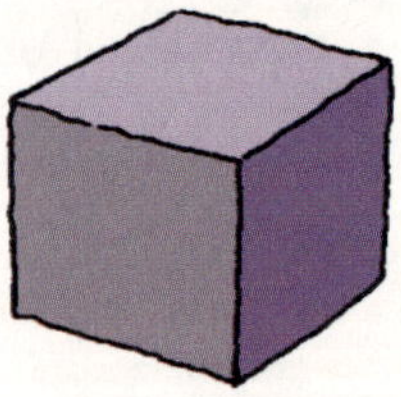

Review

Read each set of words below. **Combine** words from each set to write three complete sentences.

1

A cute cub
The mail
The seal

2

can eat
likes to go
may be

3

near the gate.
nine peas.
to the sea.

Think and Link Look at the pictures.
Read the words and pictures to make a sentence.

A  sees the  in the C.

Review

Look at each picture. **Read** the words in the box. **Write** sentences about the picture using the words in the box for help.

hike	bees	cube	wave
rail	cute	leap	note

1

2

I Can Read It!

The Window Cleaner

by M. Long

When I grow up I want to be
A window cleaning man
And make the windows in our street
As shiny as I can.
I'll put my ladder by the wall
And up the steps I'll go
But when I'm up there with my pail
I hope the wind won't blow.

Circle the two words with the long *a* sound /ā/ in the poem. **Write** the words on the line below.

Answer this question.

Why does the child in the poem hope the wind will not blow?

I Can Write It!

Think about what you might like to do when you grow up. **Draw** what you might do. **Write** about your picture.

happy	grow	make	see	use
feel	like	ride	take	way

At Home Talk about different jobs your child can think about based on his or her interests.

Someday I may work in a zoo.
Do you know what you want to do?

8

Someday

This book belongs to

1

cut

fold

I think I want to fly a plane.

6

Or write books about A to Z.

3

Someday I may sail on the sea.

2

Or maybe I will drive a train.

7

I dream of my own radio show.

4

Or helping a little puppy grow.

5

At the Store

A Grocery Trip

High on a shelf
Or way down low,
There are all kinds of things
In a store,
Don't you know?

A sample to taste,
Mother says, "Try it!"
How fun to try food out
Before you
Can buy it!

Mom's cart is full
As it goes out the door,
You can't wait to come back—
It was fun
At the store!

On My Mind

What do you like to shop for?

All-STARs at Home

Dear Family,

Our class is beginning Unit 5 of *SRA All-STAR Phonics*. The theme of this unit is "At the Store." In this unit your child will continue to learn about consonant sounds. He or she will be introduced to consonant blends, such as *bl, gr,* and *st.* Your child will learn about blends at the beginning and at the end of words. Knowing these blends will help your child read longer words.

The following fun activities can help your child become familiar with consonant blends:

★ Say one of the following words. Have your child make a new word by adding a new consonant sound.

You say: "Top."
Your child says, "Top."

You say: "Add *s* at the beginning."
Your child says, "Stop."

lap (add c) **clap,** (add s) **slap,** (add f) **flap**

rip (add d) **drip,** (add g) **grip,** (add t) **trip**

After some practice, take turns with your child so he or she can think of a word and a consonant blend.

★ Look through grocery or toy ads with your child. Ask your child to circle words he or she can read. Write these words on index cards. Sort these cards in different ways, such as by beginning letter or beginning consonant blend. Look for consonant blends in the middle of words too!

★ Look for books about going to the store in your library or bookstore. We recommend:

- *Grandpa's Corner Store* by Dyanne DiSalvo-Ryan, HarperCollins Juvenile Books, 2000.
- *Molly's Store (We Can Read!)* by Jacqueline Sweeney, Benchmark Books, 2000.

All-STAR Readers Know

A **blend** is two consonants sounded together so that each letter is heard.

/s/ /t/ /o/ /p/ → /st/ /o/ /p/ → *stop*

The underlined letters in the words below are *s* blends.

skate  *smile*  *snail* 

spoon  *stop* 

swim 

Say each picture name. **Listen** to the beginning *s* blend. **Circle** the picture if it has the same beginning *s* blend shown on its price tag.

st

sp

sn

sw

sp

sk

sp

sk

sw

I Can Do It!

Lesson 1: Introducing *s* Blends

Say each picture name. **Listen** to the beginning *s* blend. **Fill in** the circle next to each picture that begins with the same *s* blend as the top picture.

1

4

2

5

3

6

I Can Do It!

Say each picture name. **Listen** to the beginning *s* blend. **Circle** the *s* blend that stands for the sounds you hear at the beginning of the word. **Write** the *s* blend on the line.

1. 
   (sw) st sp
   sw

2. 
   sk st sp

3. 

   sp st sm

4. 
   st sn sw

5. 
   sm sn sk

6. 
   sn sk sp

7. 
   sw sp st

8. 
   sn sk sm

9. 
   sp st sw

Big Idea What does your favorite store sell?

I Can Do It!

Lesson 2: Identifying *s* Blends

Say each picture name. **Listen** to the beginning *s* blend. **Write** the correct *s* blend to complete each picture name.

sk sm sn sp st sw

1

spin

2

___ate

3

___im

4

___ile

5

___ore

6

___ap

Riddle Time What do you call a shop that sells beds?

A ___ore ___ore!

I Can Do It!

Read each word. **Fill in** the circle next to the picture that matches the word.

1 spot ●  ○  ○ 

2 snail ○  ○  ○ 

3 stone ○ 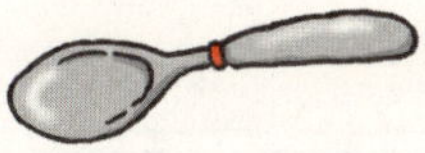 ○  ○ 

4 swim ○  ○ 

○ 

5 skate ○  ○  ○ 

6 smile ○  ○ 

○ 

Think and Link Circle all of the words that begin with an *s* blend.

People who work in stores scan items for prices. The bar codes help the stores keep track of the stuff they sell.

0 29129 00495 00028

I Can Do It!

Lesson 3: Using *s* Blends

Read each sentence. **Fill in** the circle next to the word that makes sense in the sentence. **Write** the word on the line.

1 I buy  at a store.

- (●) store
- ( ) skip
- ( ) swim

2  wore her ________.

- ( ) stays
- ( ) sweeps
- ( ) skates

3 I peel the  ________.

- ( ) skin
- ( ) stop
- ( ) smoke

4  has a nice ________.

- ( ) spot
- ( ) smile
- ( ) still

5  are on the ________.

- ( ) snap
- ( ) snake
- ( ) stove

I Can Do It!

All-STAR Readers Know

The letter *l* also can be part of a blend.

/f/ /l/ /a/ /g/ → /fl/ /a/ /g/ → *flag*

The underlined letters in the words below are *l* blends.

block  *clock*  *flute* 

glue  *plane*  *slide* 

Say each picture name. **Listen** to the beginning *l* blend. **Circle** the picture if it has the same beginning *l* blend shown on its price tag.

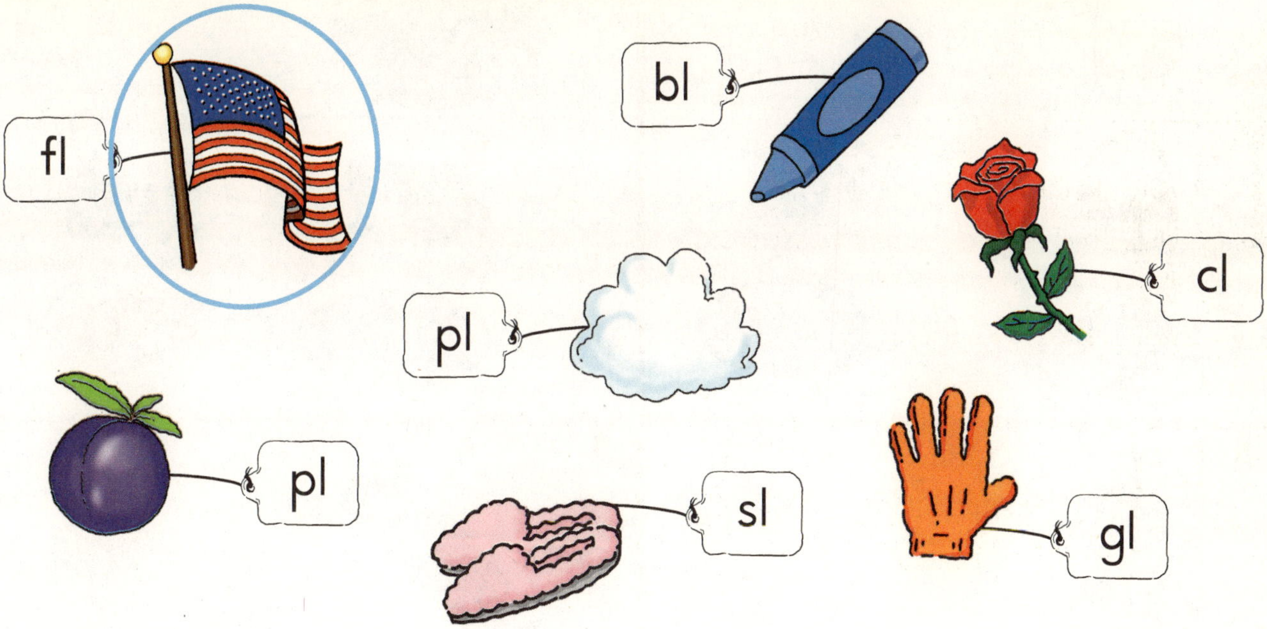

Think and Link Write three things you can buy at a pet store.

I Can Do It!

Lesson 4: Introducing l Blends

Say each picture name. Listen to the beginning l blend. Fill in the circle next to each picture that begins with the same l blend as the top picture.

1

2

3

4

5

6

I Can Do It!

Say each picture name. **Listen** to the beginning *l* blend. **Circle** the *l* blend that stands for the sounds you hear at the beginning of the word. **Write** the blend on the line.

1

bl
cl
fl

cl

2

sl
gl
fl

3

fl
sl
pl

4

gl
bl
sl

5

pl
bl
fl

6

fl
sl
gl

7

bl
cl
sl

8

cl
gl
pl

9

sl
pl
bl

Big Idea How do you think milk gets to the store?

I Can Do It!

Lesson 5: Identifying l Blends

Say each picture name. Listen to the beginning l blend. Write the correct l blend to complete each picture name.

bl   cl   fl   gl   pl   sl

1 

glue

2 

___ock

3 

___y

4 

___um

5 

___ock

6 

___ue

7 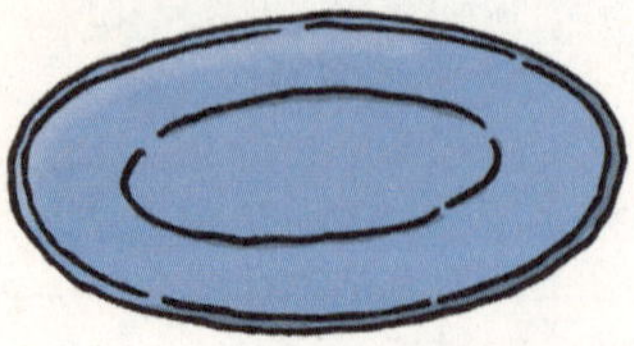

___ate

8 

___ide

9 

___ug

I Can Do It!

Read each word. **Fill in** the circle next to the picture that matches the word.

1 flag ●  ○ 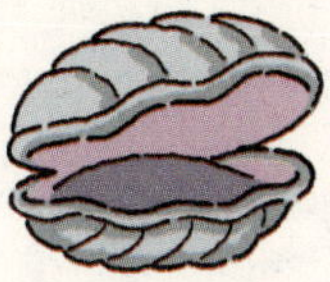 ○ 

2 sled ○  ○  ○ 

3 glue ○  ○  ○ 

4 black ○ 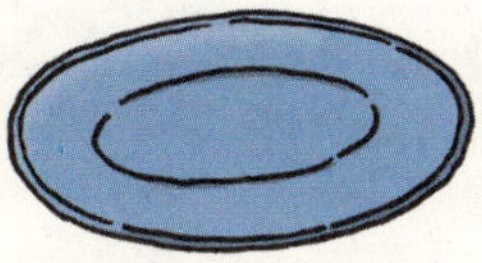 ○  ○ 

5 clock ○  ○ 

○ 

6 plate ○ 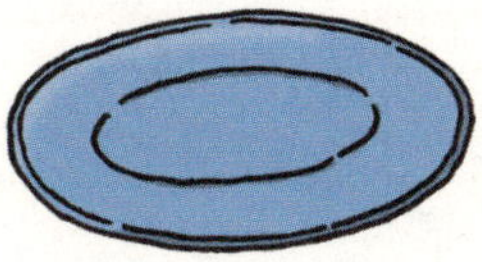 ○  ○ 

Rhyme Time Say three words that rhyme with *clay*.

I Can Do It!

Lesson 6: Using l Blends

Read each sentence. **Fill in** the circle next to the word that makes sense in the sentence. **Write** the word on the line.

1.  needs a clock.

   - ● clock
   - ○ block
   - ○ globe

2. The ______ says 

.

   - ○ clam
   - ○ flap
   - ○ flag

3. Ed is ______ to see .

   - ○ glad
   - ○ sled
   - ○ play

4. Ed has a ______ .

   - ○ black
   - ○ blue
   - ○ slide

5. It has 3 ______.

   - ○ flowers
   - ○ flies
   - ○ plugs

I Can Do It!

All-STAR Readers Know

The letter *r* can also be part of a blend.

/c/ /r/ /i/ /b/ → /cr/ /i/ /b/ → *crib*

The underlined letters in the words below are *r* blends.

brick  *crib*  *dress* 

frog  *green*  *train* 

Say each picture name. **Listen** to the beginning *r* blend. **Circle** the picture if it has the same beginning *r* blend shown on its price tag.

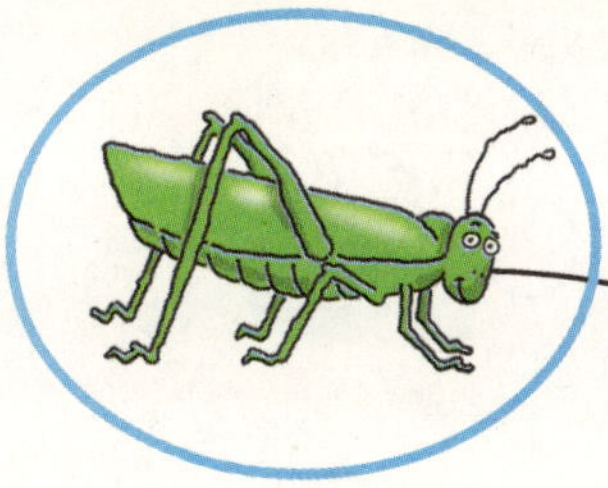 gr

 br

 pr

 cr

 fr

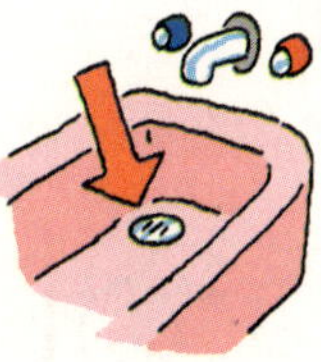 dr

 dr

 cr

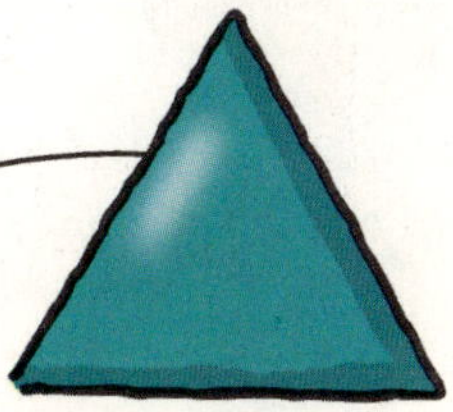 tr

I Can Do It!

Lesson 7: Introducing *r* Blends

Say each picture name. **Listen** to the beginning *r* blend. **Fill in** the circle next to each picture that begins with the same *r* blend as the top picture.

1

4

2

5

3

6

I Can Do It!

Say each picture name. **Listen** to the beginning *r* blend. **Circle** the *r* blend that stands for the sounds you hear at the beginning of the word. **Write** the blend on the line.

1. 
   br
   cr
   dr
   cr

2. 
   tr
   br
   fr

3. 
   fr
   tr
   gr

4. 
   dr
   fr
   br

5. 
   tr
   br
   fr

6. 
   gr
   tr
   cr

7. 
   fr
   gr
   br

8. 
   cr
   fr
   br

9. 
   cr
   br
   dr

Tongue Twister Six trick brick trucks.

I Can Do It!

Lesson 8: Identifying *r* Blends

Say each picture name. **Listen** to the beginning *r* blend. **Write** the correct *r* blend to complete each picture name.

br cr dr fr gr tr

1 

gr een

2 

___ ame

3 

___ ain

4 

___ ush

5 

___ ick

6 

___ ess

7 

___ ab

8 

___ ee

9 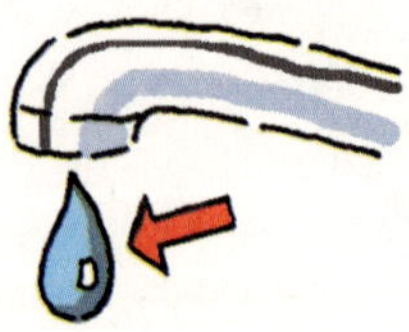

___ ip

I Can Do It!

Read each word. **Fill in** the circle next to the picture that matches the word.

1 braid

● 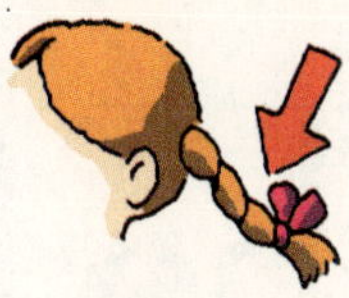 ○  ○ 

2 tray

○  ○ 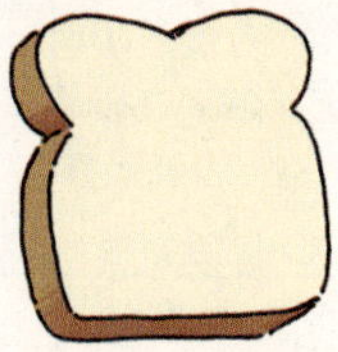 ○ 

3 grill

○  ○  ○ 

4 frog

○  ○  ○ 

5 drum

○  ○  ○ 

6 frame

○  ○  ○ 

Big Idea If you had a store, what would you like to sell?

Lesson 9: Using *r* Blends

Read each sentence. **Fill in** the circle next to the word that makes sense in the sentence. **Write** the word on the line.

1 Jo drove to the 

.

- ● drove
- ○ smile
- ○ slide

2 She ________ red .

- ○ drain
- ○ green
- ○ grows

3  ________ a fresh one.

- ○ spill
- ○ tries
- ○ drill

4 He buys 4 ________.

- ○ cry
- ○ true
- ○ crates

5  is ________ of them.

- ○ proud
- ○ crowd
- ○ frog

I Can Do It!

All-STAR Readers Know

Blends can also come at the end of words. The underlined letters in the words below are ending blends.

sta<u>mp</u>  *te<u>nt</u>*  *ma<u>sk</u>* 

Say the name of each picture. **Listen** for the blend at the **end** of the word. **Draw** a line from the picture to the blend you hear at the **end** of the word.

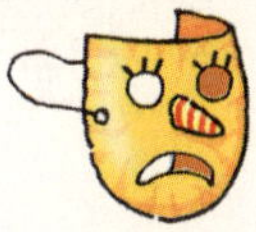

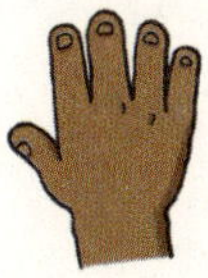

mp

nd

nk

nt

sk

st

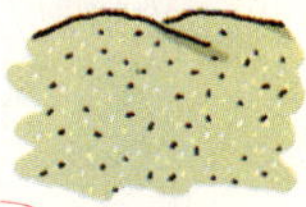

Joke Corner What do you buy for a bug? A pe___ ve___!

I Can Do It!

Lesson 10: Introducing Ending Blends

Say each picture name. **Listen** for the blend at the **end** of the word. **Fill in** the circle next to each picture that has the same **ending blend** as the top picture.

1

4

2

5

3

6

I Can Do It!

Say each picture name. Listen for the blend at the **end** of the word. Circle the blend you hear at the **end** of the word. Write the blend on the line.

1 
mp
st
nt

mp

2 
nk
sk
st

3 
st
nt
mp

4 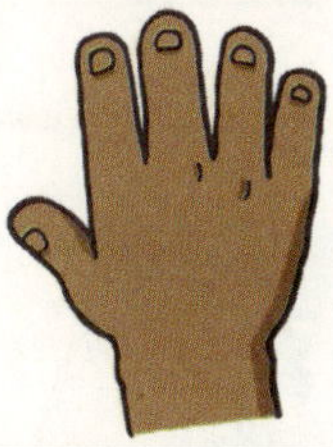
st
nd
nt

5 
nt
mp
st

6 

sk
mp
st

7 
st
sk
nt

8 
nk
nd
sk

9 
nd
nk
sk

Think and Link Name some stores in your city. Which ones have blends in their names?

I Can Do It!

Lesson 11: Identifying Ending Blends

Say each picture name. Listen for the blend at the end of the word. Write the correct ending blend to complete each picture name.

mp nd nk nt sk st

1 

sta**mp**

2 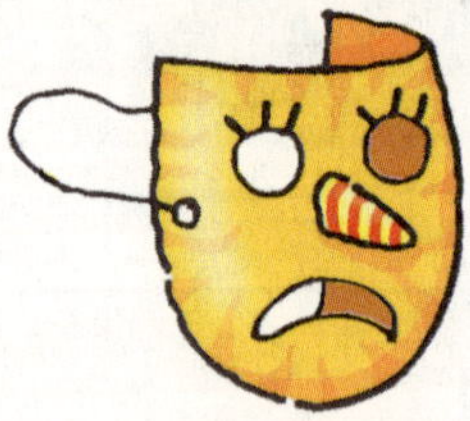

ma___

3 

sa___

4 

ve___

5 

po___

6 

te___

7 

si___

8 

pla___

9 

sku___

Review

Read each word. **Fill in** the circle below the word that names the picture. **Circle** the blend.

1

grass ○ globe ○ green ○

4

stamp ○ stick ○ lamp ○

2

flame ○ frame ○ fan ○

5

plane ○ pan ○ plant ○

3

list ○ rain ○ train ○

6

spin ○ skunk ○ trunk ○

Tongue Twister Six young skunks stunk.

Review

Lesson 12: Review Blends

Say each picture name.
Write the picture name on the line.

hand	flag	glue	skate	swim
desk	sink	lamp	green	

1 

____

2 

____

3 

____

4 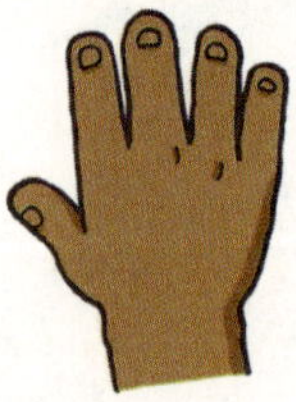

____

5 

____

6 

____

7 

____

8 

____

9 

____

I Can Read It!

Blend and Spend

Dad took me to the store,
He gave me lots to spend,
But I could only buy the things
That started with a blend.

So...

I got
glue
skates
stew
plates
flies
drapes
fries
grapes
black slacks
green snacks
crushed prunes
clean spoons

Now I'm broke, so that's the end.

Underline each word in the poem that begins with a blend.

I Can Write It!

Lesson 14: Writing

Imagine that you are going to the store.
Draw a picture of what you need to buy.
Write your shopping list on the lines.

br cl gr nt pl sk sl st tr

From the Store

At Home Ask your child to help you write the shopping list the next time you go to the store. He or she can also circle the words with beginning or ending blends.

My baby brother just smiles and claps.
The big, new store is a special place!

The Big, New Store

This book belongs to

We buy glue, clay, and
crayons for school.

My little sister likes green grapes.

We went to the big, new store.

2

My sister asks for a frog book.

7

I want a sweet apple to taste.

4

Mom smells fresh bread.

5

Unit 6 Consonant Digraphs

At the Seashore

Fish

by Mary Ann Hoberman

Look at them flit
Lickety-split
Wiggling
Swiggling
Swerving
Curving
Hurrying
Scurrying
Chasing
Racing
Whizzing
Whisking
Flying
Frisking
Tearing around
With a leap and a bound
But none of them making the tiniest
tiniest
tiniest
tiniest
sound.

On My Mind

What other animals live in the sea?

All-STARs at Home

Dear Family,

Our class is beginning Unit 6 of *SRA All-STAR Phonics*. Your child will be studying consonant digraphs while learning about the theme, "At the Seashore." A consonant digraph is two consonants that stand for a new sound when they are together in a word. The boldfaced letters in the words below are examples of consonant digraphs:

sh**ell* *too**th *pea**ch*** ***kn**ee* ***wh**ite*

The following fun activities can help your child become familiar with these sounds.

★ Say a word and ask your child to make a list of rhyming words. For example, encourage your child to start with *fish* and give rhymes such as *wish, dish,* and *squish.* They can do the same thing with *match* and *path.*

★ Play the "Digraph Shell Game." Write these digraphs on small pieces of paper: *ch, sh, th.* Hide each piece of paper under a cup (not a glass). Have your child uncover one at a time. He or she says three words that begin with that digraph. Vary the game by telling your child three words that contain that digraph and he or she tells you if the digraph comes at the beginning, middle, or end of the word.

★ Look for books about the seashore in the library or bookstore. We suggest:

- *Sally Goes to the Beach* by Stephen Huneck, Harry N. Abrams, 2000.
- *On My Beach There Are Many Pebbles* by Leo Lionni, Mulberry Books, 1995.

I Can Do It!

All-STAR Readers Know

When the letters *sh* are together in a word, they stand for the sound heard at the beginning of *shell.*

Say each picture name. **Write** *sh* next to the pictures that begin with the /sh/ sound. **Write** *s* next to the pictures that begin with the /s/ sound.

1

sh

2

3

4

5

6

7

8

9

Tongue Twister She sells sea shells by the seashore.

I Can Do It!

Lesson 1: Beginning *sh*

Say each picture name. Circle the word that names the picture. Write the picture name on the line.

1

shell shed

shell

2

shape skate

3

shake snake

4

ship slip

5

shed sled

6

sheep sleep

7

shop stop

8

show soap

9

shut sun

All-STAR Readers Know

When the letters *th* are together in a word, they often stand for the sound heard at the beginning of *thumb*. 

Say each picture name. **Write** *th* next to the pictures that begin with the /th/ sound. **Write** *t* next to the pictures that begin with the /t/ sound.

1 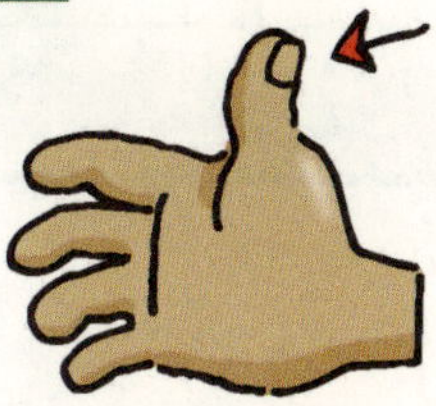 th

2  ______

3  ______

4  ______

5  ______

6 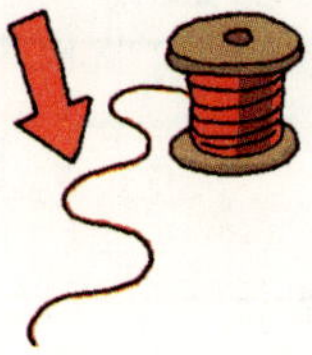 ______

7  ______

8  ______

9  ______

Think and Link What do all seashores share?

___e___ide!

I Can Do It!

Lesson 2: Beginning *th*

Say each picture name. Fill in the circle next to the word that names the picture. Write the picture name on the line.

1

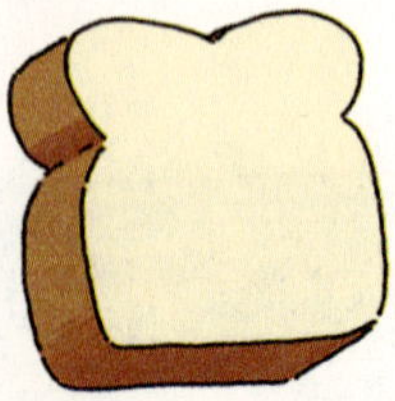

● thick ○ trick

thick

2

○ thorn ○ torn

3

○ three ○ tree

4

○ them ○ tent

5

○ thin ○ tin

6

○ throw ○ tow

7

○ thorn ○ torn

8

○ then ○ ten

9

○ think ○ tank

Review

Say each picture name. **Circle** the letters that stand for the sound you hear at the beginning of each picture name. **Write** the letters on the line.

1

sh th

2

sh th

3

sh th

4

sh th

5

sh th

6

sh th

7

sh th

8
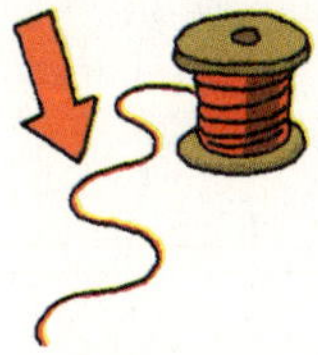
sh th

9

sh th

Review

Lesson 3: Review Beginning *sh, th*

Read each sentence. **Choose** a word from the box that makes sense in the sentence. **Complete** the sentence.

show	shell	shape	Then	think

1 I had a big shell.

2 Its ________ was neat.

3 I ________ I'll play.

4 I want to ________ you.

5 ________ I will swim.

All-STAR Readers Know

When the letters *ch* are together in a word, they often stand for the sound heard at the beginning of *cheese.*

Say each picture name. **Write** *ch* next to the pictures that start with the /ch/ sound. **Write** *c* next to the pictures that start with the sound of *c*.

1  ch

2 

3 

4 

5 

6 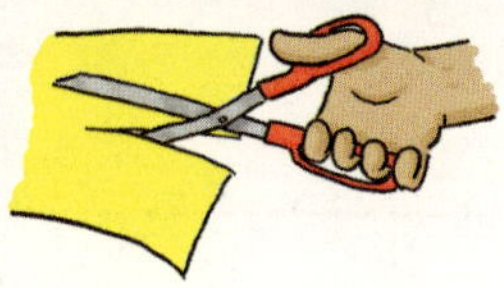

7 

8 

9 

On-Track Fact Coral looks like a rock, but it is really alive! Many tiny animals live together in a coral reef.

I Can Do It!

Lesson 4: Beginning *ch*

Say each picture name. Circle the word that names the picture. Write the picture name on the line.

1

chick click

chick

2

cheek creek

3

cane crane

4

cheese cream

5

chin clip

6

chat cat

7

chair care

8

chase cake

9

chop hop

I Can Do It!

All-STAR Readers Know

When the letters *wh* are together in a word, they often stand for the sound heard at the beginning of *wheel.*

Say each picture. Fill in the circle under each picture that begins with the /hw/ sound.

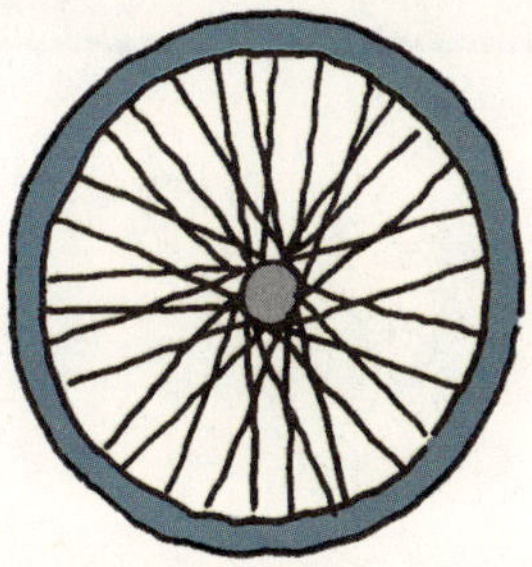

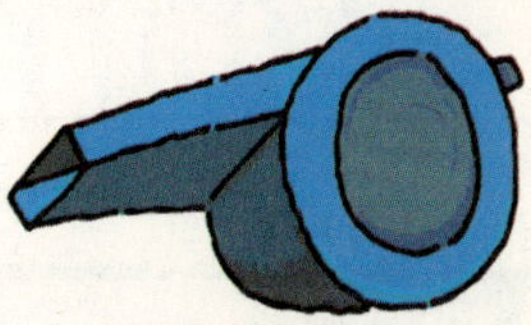

On-Track Fact A whale is a mammal that lives in the sea, but it breathes air just like you.

I Can Do It!

Lesson 5: Beginning *wh*

Say each picture name. **Fill in** the circle next to the word that names the picture. **Write** the picture name on the line.

1

● white ○ wipe

white

2

○ whip ○ wig

3

○ wheat ○ meat

4

○ wheel ○ well

5

○ whale ○ wave

6

○ when ○ hen

7

○ whip ○ win

8

○ white ○ hit

9

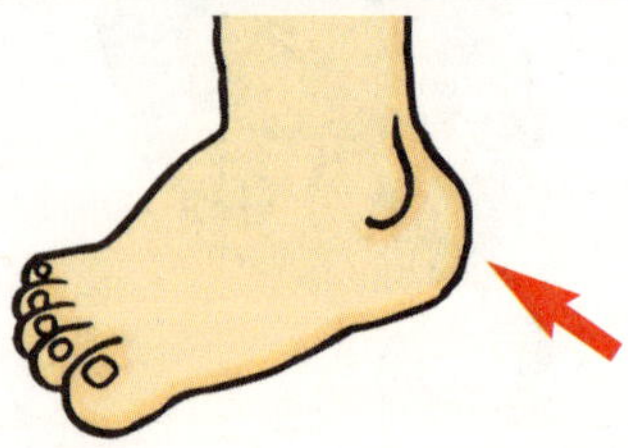

○ wheel ○ heel

I Can Do It!

All-STAR Readers Know

When the letters *kn* are together in a word, they stand for the /n/ sound, as in *knee.* 

Say each picture name. Write *kn* next to each picture that begins with the /n/ sound. Write *k* next to each picture that begins with the /k/ sound.

1  kn

2 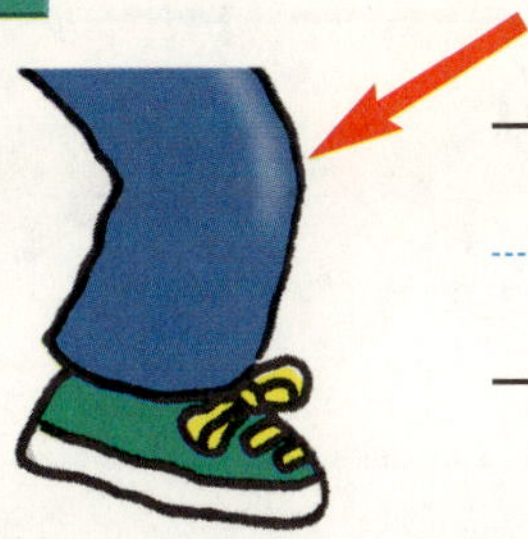

3 

4 

5 

6 

7 

8 

9 

On-Track Fact What makes waves in the ocean? Most waves are caused by wind that blows over the water.

Lesson 6: Beginning *kn*

Read the word.
Circle the picture that matches the word.

1 knife

2 knee

3 knot

 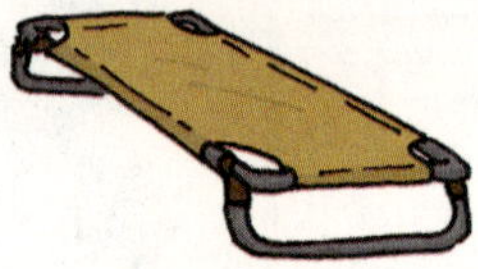 

4 knob

  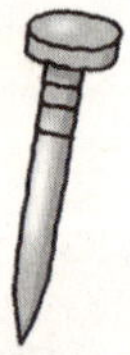

5 knit

6 knock

Think and Link How many knees does an octopus have?

Answer: None! An octopus has eight arms but no legs.

Review

Say each picture name. **Circle** the letters that stand for the sound you hear at the beginning of each word. **Write** the letters on the line.

1

ch kn wh

wh

2

ch kn wh

3

ch kn wh

4

ch kn wh

5
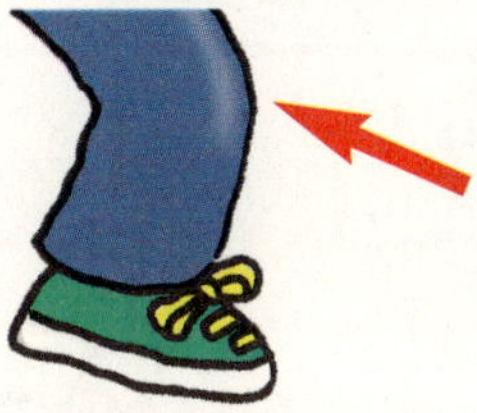
ch kn wh

6

ch kn wh

7

ch kn wh

8

ch kn wh

9

ch kn wh

Review

Lesson 7: Review Beginning *ch, wh, kn*

Say each picture name. **Read** the words in the box. **Write** each picture name on the line.

whale	knit	chick	white	cheese
knot	chair	knife	wheel	

1

____

2

____

3

____

4

____

5

____

6

____

7

____

8

____

9

____

I Can Do It!

All-STAR Readers Know

The letters *sh* can also come at the end of a word.

Say each picture name. **Circle** the picture if its name **ends** with the /sh/ sound.

Joke Corner What is the most famous animal in the sea?

The starfi___!

I Can Do It!

Lesson 8: Ending *sh*

Say each picture name. **Write** *sh* on the line if the picture name **ends** with the /sh/ sound.

1

sh

2

3

4

5

6
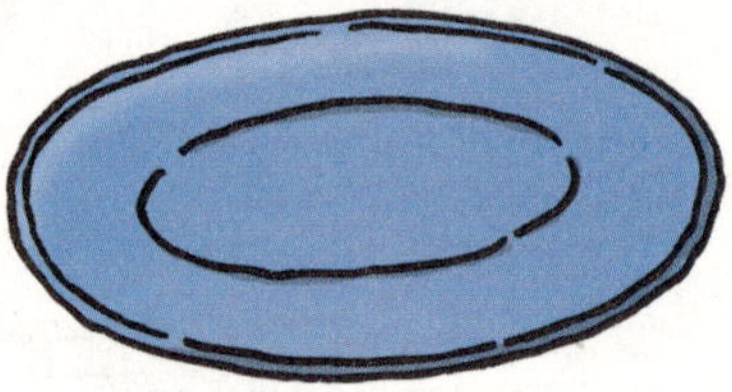

7

8

9
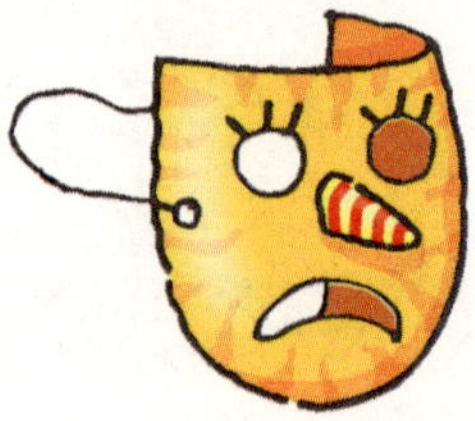

On-Track Fact The deepest part of the ocean is about seven miles deep!

I Can Do It!

All-STAR Readers Know

The letters *th* can also come at the end of a word.

Say each picture name. Circle the picture if its name **ends** with the /th/ sound.

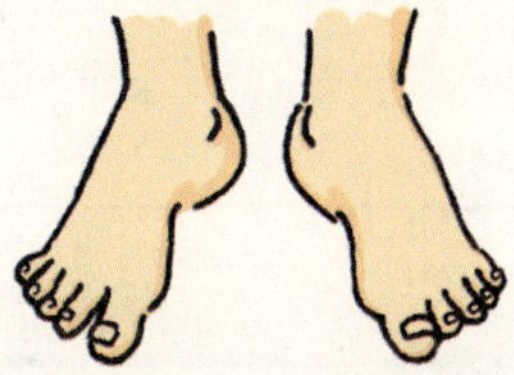

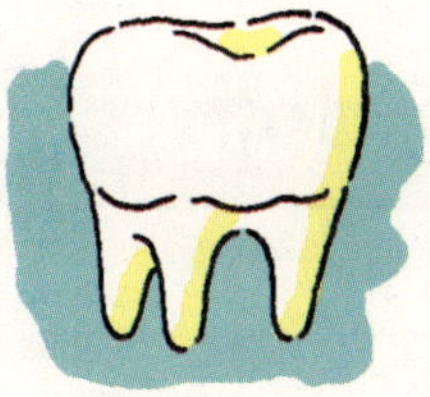

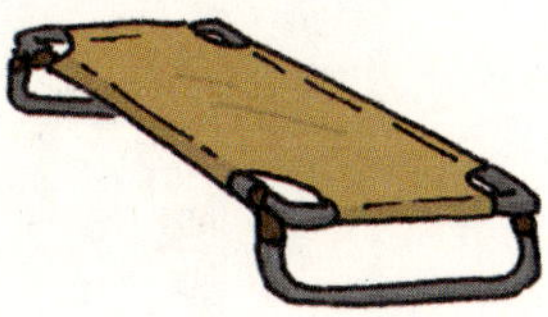

Big Idea Did you know there are five oceans? Look on a map and try to find all of them.

I Can Do It!

Lesson 9: Ending *th*

Say each picture name. **Fill in** the circle next to the word that names the picture. **Write** the picture name on the line if it **ends** with the /th/ sound.

1

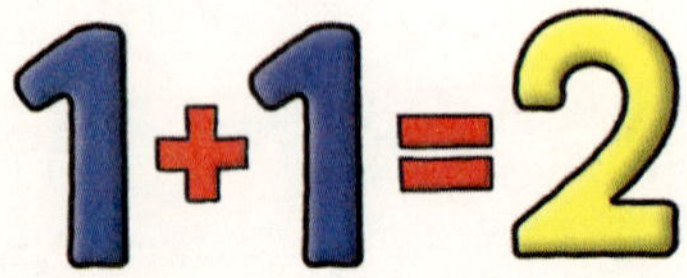

● math ○ mat

math

2

○ both ○ boat

3

○ bath ○ bat

4

○ moth ○ mom

5

○ with ○ whip

6

○ path ○ pat

7

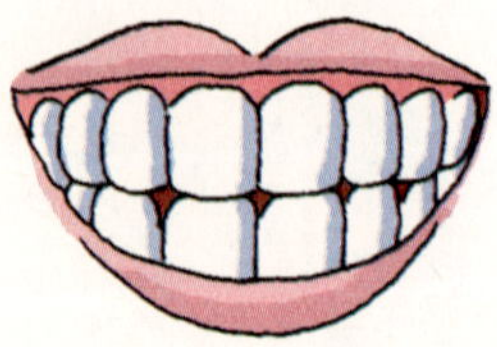

○ teeth ○ team

8

○ cloth ○ clock

9

○ truth ○ truck

I Can Do It!

All-STAR Readers Know

The letters *ch* can also come at the end of a word.

Say each picture name. **Circle** the picture if its name **ends** with the /ch/ sound.

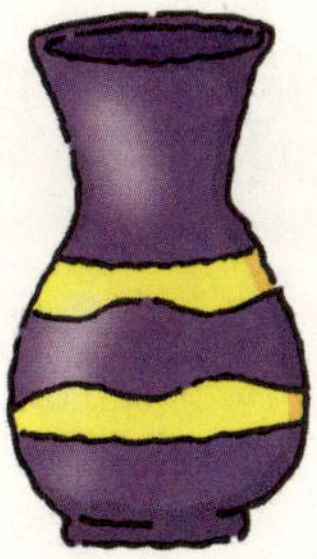

On-Track Fact A seahorse father carries his babies in a pouch.

I Can Do It!

Lesson 10: Ending *ch*

Say each picture name. **Fill in** the circle next to the word that names the picture. **Write** the picture name on the line if it ends with the /ch/ sound.

1

● bench ○ bed

bench

2

○ lunch ○ lamp

3

○ beach ○ bell

4

○ inch ○ ink

5

○ bunch ○ bank

6

○ reach ○ read

7

○ ranch ○ rake

8

○ branch ○ brick

9

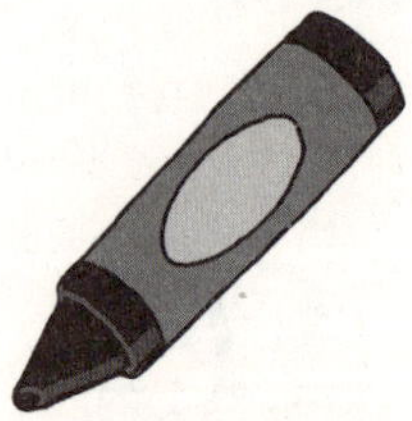

○ black ○ bleach

Review

Say each picture name. **Circle** the letters that stand for the sound at the **end** of each word. **Write** the letters on the line.

1 

ch sh (th)

th

2 

ch sh th

3 

ch sh th

4 

ch sh th

5 

ch sh th

6 

ch sh th

7 

ch sh th

8 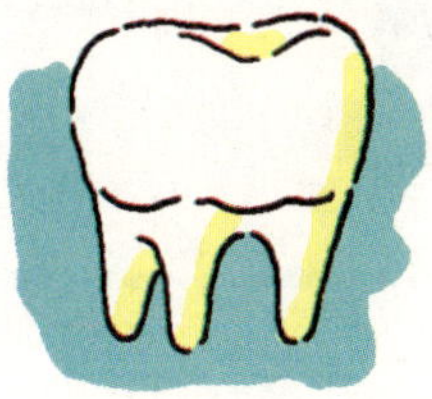

ch sh th

9 

ch sh th

On-Track Fact Most shells are homes to small animals.

Review

Lesson 11: Review Ending *sh, th, ch*

Read the word.
Circle the picture that matches the word.

1 brush

2 dish

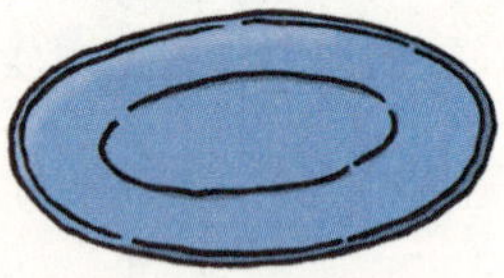  

3 beach

4 moth

  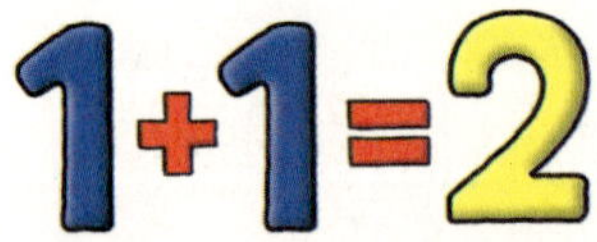

5 tooth

  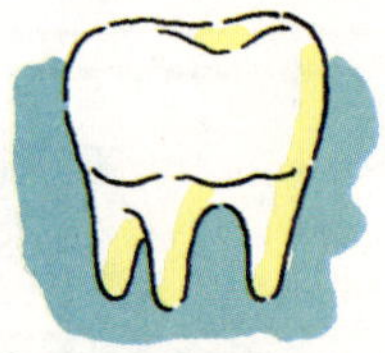

6 fish

On-Track Fact Many birds live near the seashore.

Driving to the Beach

by Joanna Cole

On the road
Smell the fumes and tar
through the windows
of the car.

But at the beach
smell suntan lotion
and wind
and sun
and ocean!

Circle the word in the poem that has an *sh*, *th*, or *ch* ending. **Write** the word on the line.

What are some things you might hear at the beach?

I Can Write It!

Lesson 13: Writing

Draw a picture of yourself at the beach.
Write about your picture on the lines.
The words in the box may help you.

beach	swim	splash	crab
shells	sand	fish	float

At Home Ask your child to tell you about his or her drawing. Then have your child circle anything in the drawing with the /sh/ sound.

Hooray! We are going to the beach!

8

A Wish

This book belongs to

1

cut

I wish I could watch for whales.

6

I wish I could jump in the waves.

3

fold

cut

I wish I could go on a trip.

2

I like to look for shells.

4

I wish I could swim in the sea.

5

I like to play in the sand.

7

All about Time

Daylight Saving Time

by Phyllis McGinley

In Spring when maple buds are red,
We turn the Clock an hour ahead;
Which means, each April that arrives,
We lose an hour
Out of our lives.

Who cares? When Autumn birds in flocks
Fly southward, back we turn the Clocks,
And so regain a lovely thing—
That missing hour
We lost last Spring.

On My Mind

What would be different if we did not use Daylight Saving Time?

All-STARs at Home

Dear Family,

Our class is beginning Unit 7 of *SRA All-STAR Phonics*. The theme of this final unit is "All about Time." We will be learning about parts of words, such as the endings *-s* and *-es*, which can change a word from singular to plural; the ending *-ed*, which tells about the past; and the ending *-ing*, which tells about something that is happening right now. We will work with compound words, which are made by putting together two small words, as in the word *seashell*. We will also learn about contractions. We make contractions by putting together two words and then leaving out some letters in order to make a smaller word. For example, *do* and *not* can form the contraction *don't*.

Here are some fun activities that will help your child become familiar with word endings:

★ As you read stories with your child, point out words that have the inflectional endings *-s, -ed,* and *-ing*. Read the word with your child and ask him or her to tell you what ending is on each word.

★ Make compound-word cards. Write compound words, such as *hotdog, cupcake, rainbow,* and *backpack*, on cards. Cut the two words apart. Display the cards on a table. Ask your child to put the words together to make compound words. Then ask your child to make some new compound-word cards.

★ Look for books about time in the library or bookstore. We recommend:

- *Telling Time: How to Tell Time on Digital and Analog Clocks!* by Jules Older, Charlesbridge Publishing, 2000.
- *Felix Travels Back in Time: Includes Six Pull-Out Letters and Fold-Out Map and Time Line* by Annette Langen, Abbeville Press, Inc., 1995.

I Can Do It!

All-STAR Readers Know

A **plural** is a word that means more than one. To make a word plural, you usually add *s*.

cat ➜ *cats*

Read the words. **Draw** a line from the picture to the word that names each picture.

1 chick   chicks

2 cat   cats

3 hand 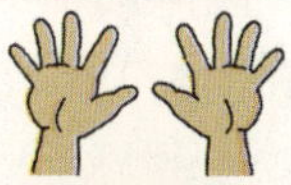 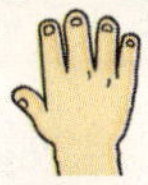 hands

4 duck   ducks

5 rake   rakes

6 boat   boats

I Can Do It!

Lesson 1: Plurals with -s

Say each picture name. **Look** at the words in the box. **Write** the picture name on the line. **Add** *s* to the picture name if it shows more than one.

tree	hat	pig	tent	grape
bike	pail	dog	ring	

1 

hats

2 

3 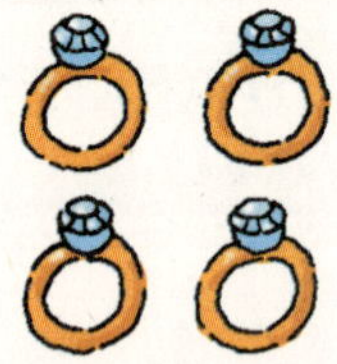

4 

5 

6 

7 

8 

9 

I Can Do It!

All-STAR Readers Know

When a word ends with *ch, sh, s,* or *x,* add *es* to make the word plural.

watch → *watches* *bus* → *buses*

brush → *brushes* *fox* → *foxes*

Look at each picture. **Fill in** the circle in front of the word that names the picture. **Write** the word on the line.

1

○ box ● boxes

boxes

2

○ dish ○ dishes

3

○ brush ○ brushes

4

○ fox ○ foxes

5

○ class ○ classes

6

○ lunch ○ lunches

7

○ flash ○ flashes

8

○ beach ○ beaches

9

○ peach ○ peaches

I Can Do It!

Read each sentence. **Circle** the word that best completes each sentence. **Write** the word on the line.

1 

She fed the dogs.

(dogs) boxes

2 

We eat ________.

logs lunches

3 

Al trims ________.

trees watches

4 

She has two ________.

cats brushes

5 

Pick up the ________.

twins dishes

Riddle Time Circle the plural words in this riddle. What has hands but no arms?

Answer: A clock!

I Can Do It!

All-STAR Readers Know

The ending *-s* means the action is happening now.

play + s → plays *run + s → runs*

Read each word. **Write** a new word on the line by adding the ending *s*.

1 ride rides

2 think ______

3 sleep ______

4 run ______

5 eat ______

6 see ______

Write two sentences about time using two of the new words you wrote above.

7 ______

8 ______

I Can Do It!

Read each sentence. **Find** the word from the box below that best completes each sentence. **Write** the word that makes sense in the sentence on the line. Hint: Use each word only once.

puts	throws	wags	runs	plays	says

1 Spot ________ his tail.

2 Peg ________ food down.

3 Peg ________ with Spot.

4 Peg ________ the ball.

5 Spot ________ to get it.

6 Peg ________ "bye."

I Can Do It!

All-STAR Readers Know

The ending *-ed* means the action has happened in the past.

jump + ed → jumped

Read each word. **Write** a new word on the line by adding the ending *ed*.

1 lock locked

2 rain

3 fix

4 clean

5 brush

6 drill

Write two sentences about time using two of the new words you wrote above.

7

8

I Can Do It!

Lesson 4: Inflectional Ending *-ed*

Read each sentence. **Find** the word from the box below that best completes each sentence. **Write** the word that makes sense in the sentence on the line.

dressed	rushed	waved
buzzed	jumped	fixed

1. The clock ________.

2. Ted ________ from bed.

3. He got ________.

4. He ________ his oatmeal.

5. He ________ to the bus.

6. He ________ good-bye.

On-Track Fact The earth travels around the sun. It takes one year to go all the way around.

I Can Do It!

All-STAR Readers Know

The ending *-ing* means the action is happening now.

jump + ing → jumping

Read each word. **Write** a new word on the line by adding the ending *ing.*

1 stay staying

2 see

3 sweep

4 mix

5 read

6 sleep

Write two sentences about time using two of the new words you wrote above.

7

8

I Can Do It!

Read each sentence. **Find** the word from the box below that best completes each sentence. **Write** the word that makes sense in the sentence on the line.

falling fishing blowing helping

1 The snow is ________.

2 Ann is ________.

3 We go ________.

4 The wind is ________.

Big Idea A clock measures the seconds, minutes, and hours in a day. What measures the days, weeks, and months in a year? ________

Review

Read the first word in each row.
Write new words by adding the endings *ed* and *ing*.

base word	word + *ed*	word + *ing*
help	helped	helping
jump		
wink	winked	
lock		
paint		painting
heat		
spill		

Review

Lesson 6: Review Inflectional Endings

Fill in the circle next to the sentence that tells about the picture. **Write** the words from both sentences that have the endings *-s, -ed,* or *-ing* on the line.

1

- ● Mitch played on the swing.
- ○ Mitch is playing with Sam.

played playing

2

- ○ Greg paints the sun.
- ○ Greg painted a cloud.

3

- ○ Beth is waiting by the trees.
- ○ Beth waits on the beach.

4

- ○ Jane is fishing with her Mom.
- ○ Jane fished with Ken.

I Can Do It!

All-STAR Readers Know

A **compound word** is made when two words are joined together to make a new word.

rain + bow ➜ rainbow *book + store ➜ bookstore*

Say each picture name. **Find** the two words in the boxes below that go together to make a compound word. **Write** the compound word on the line.

1  rainbow

2 

3 

4 

5 

rain	bow
cup	shell
hair	brush
tea	cake
sea	pot

I Can Do It!

Lesson 7: Compound Words

Say each picture name. **Find** the two words in the boxes below that go together to make a compound word. **Write** the compound word on the line.

1  snowflake

2  ____________

3 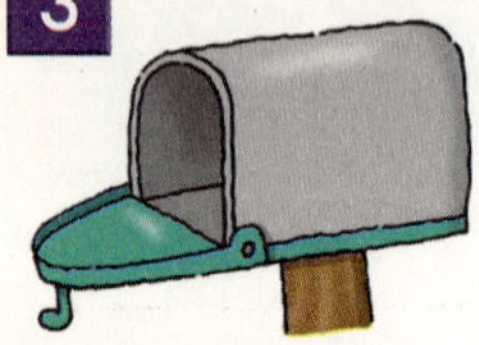 ____________

4  ____________

5  ____________

6  ____________

7  ____________

snow	flake
sail	boat
sun	meal
paint	shine
rain	box
hot	brush
oat	bow
mail	dog

I Can Do It!

Read each sentence. **Circle** the compound word in each one. **Write** the compound word on the line. **Draw** a line between the two smaller words that make up the compound word.

1 Pam put on her raincoat.

rain/coat

2 Then she went out to the backyard.

3 The raindrops stopped.

4 The sunshine lit up the sky.

5 Pam saw a rainbow.

Lesson 7: Compound Words

Read each sentence. **Fill in** the circle in front of the word that best completes the sentence. **Write** the word on the line.

1 Miko plays hopscotch.

● hopscotch ○ haystack

2 Bill has a ______________.

○ lunchbox ○ skateboard

3 Bill wears ______________.

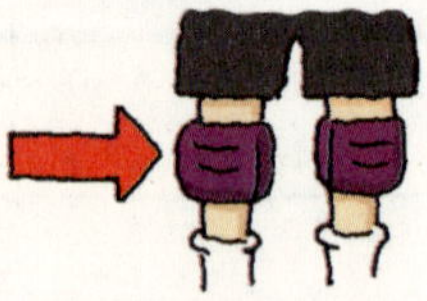

○ kneepads ○ notebooks

4 Now it is ______________.

○ lunchbox ○ lunchtime

I Can Do It!

All-STAR Readers Know

A **contraction** is made when two words are put together to make a shorter word. In a contraction some letters are left out. An *apostrophe* (') goes where the letters are missing.

he + is → he's   I + am → I'm   we + are → we're

Read each sentence. **Look** at the **boldfaced** contraction. **Write** the two words that make up the contraction on the line.

1  **I'm** happy today. I am

2 

It's my birthday. ______

3 

Mom's making a cake. ______

4  **I'm** helping her mix it. ______

5  **We're** going to eat it. ______

6  Then **it's** time for gifts. ______

I Can Do It!

Read the **boldfaced** words.
Change those words into a contraction.
Write the contraction on the line.

1 she is she's

2 we are ______

3 Mom is ______

4 he is ______

5 I am ______

6 they are ______

7 Dad is ______

8 you are ______

9 it is ______

10 Zack is ______

Riddle Time

I'm a little animal. I like to play around clocks. They're fun to run up and down. I like to say "hickory, dickory, dock." What am I?

______

I Can Do It!

All-STAR Readers Know

The words *will* and *not* can be shortened as part of a **contraction.**

do + not → don't *is + not → isn't*

he + will → he'll *I + will → I'll*

One contraction changes its spelling.

will + not → won't

Read each contraction. **Fill in** the circle next to the pair of words that make up the contraction.

1 he'll
- ○ he will
- ○ he is

2 isn't
- ○ is he
- ○ is not

3 can't
- ○ can go
- ○ can not

4 she'll
- ○ she will
- ○ she is

5 I'll
- ○ I am
- ○ I will

6 you'll
- ○ you are
- ○ you will

7 didn't
- ○ did not
- ○ do not

8 we'll
- ○ we are
- ○ we will

9 they'll
- ○ they are
- ○ they will

On-Track Fact It's true that a broken clock is right twice a day. Why?

I Can Do It!

Lesson 9: Contractions with *will, not*

Read each sentence. **Circle** the contraction that best completes the sentence. **Write** the contraction on the line.

1 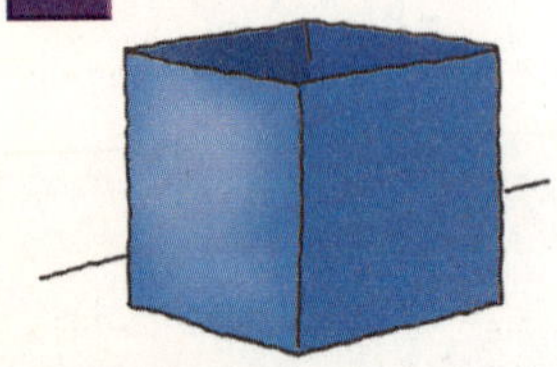

The box isn't shut.

(isn't) aren't

2 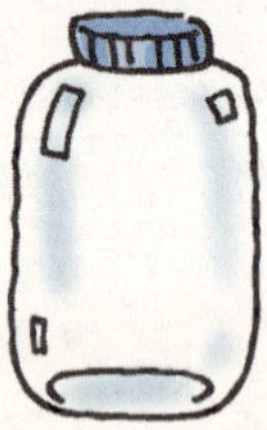

________ get a jar.

We'll Isn't

3 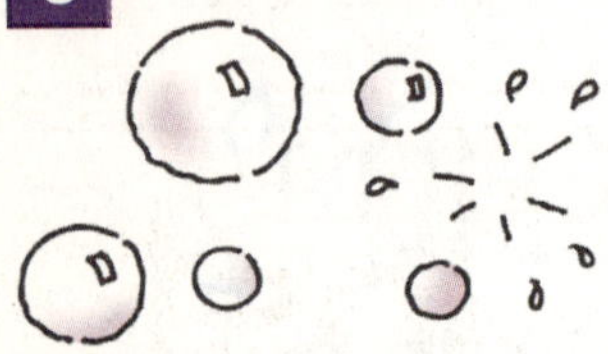

________ pop now.

They'll Can't

4 

________ have fun.

He'll She'll

5 

A frog ________ fly.

can't isn't

6 

________ cross yet.

Didn't Don't

Review

Read each sentence. **Fill in** the circle next to the word that best completes the sentence. **Write** the word on the line.

1 

I ______ find it.

○ can't ○ don't ○ isn't

2 

It's my ______.

○ fireplace ○ wristwatch ○ sunshine

3 

I hope it ______ lost.

○ isn't ○ can't ○ you're

4 

It was ______.

○ suntan ○ peanut ○ outside

5 

______ Mom great?

○ I'm ○ They're ○ Isn't

Big Idea Have you ever lost something and then found it?

Review

Lesson 10: Review Compound Words and Contractions

Read each sentence. **Circle** each compound word. **Underline** each contraction.

1 Stan and Buddy are in the backyard.

2 They're playing fetch.

3 Buddy can't catch the bone.

4 He's happy to chase it.

5 Soon Stan will get his lunchbox.

6 He'll put on his backpack.

7 Then he'll go to school.

8 Buddy will stay in his doghouse.

9 When Stan comes home, they'll be playmates again.

10 Buddy knows it's almost suppertime.

On-Track Fact Circle the three plural words in these sentences.

One day is 24 hours long. One week has 7 days. That means there are 168 hours in a week!

I Can Read It!

Bad Timing

by Arden Davidson

My watch is broken
so I can't tell time.
I don't know if it's midnight
or quarter past nine.

I don't know if I'm eating
my dinner or lunch.
I don't know if I should be
in bed or at brunch.

I've broken my watch
and I haven't a clue
what in the world
I am supposed to do.

What time could it be?
I hope that it's three
because that's when my favorite
cartoon's on TV.

I think I hear the school bells
and if that's the case,
I'm in the right time
but I'm in the wrong place!

Read the poem. **Circle** the contractions. Then answer the question below.

How can you know what time it is if your watch is broken?

I Can Write It!

Lesson 12: Writing

Draw a picture of what you like to do during your favorite time of year. **Write** about your picture on the lines below. **Use** the words in the box for help.

skateboard	springtime	we're	it's
summertime	playmates	fall	
sometimes	winter	I'll	

At Home Discuss the following words that describe time with your child: *weekend*, *summertime*, *months*, *seasons*, and *minutes*.

We'll never be too early or too late again!

Too Early, Too Late

This book belongs to

____

I'll never be late for another baseball game!

I missed my best friend's birthday party because I didn't know when noon was.

It's important to tell time!

2

I helped Mom get my little sister to dancing lessons on time.

7

One time, I showed up with my baseball bat and glove two hours early!

4

Now I can tell time from sunrise to sunset!

5

Photo Credits

Practice Page

Use this page for extra writing and drawing practice.

Practice Page

Use this page for extra writing and drawing practice.

Practice Page

Use this page for extra writing and drawing practice.

Practice Page

Use this page for extra writing and drawing practice.

Practice Page

Use this page for extra writing and drawing practice.

Practice Page

Use this page for extra writing and drawing practice.